Also by Florence Rome

THE SCARLETT LETTERS

FLORENCE ROME

*An American woman reports
on the Japanese
criminal underworld*

THE
TATTOOED
MEN

DELACORTE PRESS / NEW YORK

Manufactured in the United States of America

First printing

Designed by MaryJane DiMassi

Library of Congress Cataloging in Publication Data

Rome, Florence.
The tattooed men.

Bibliography: p.
1. Crime and criminals—Japan. 2. Gangs—Japan.
3. Organized crime—Japan. I. Title.
HV7112.R6   364.1′06′052   74-26799

ISBN 0-440-05960-7

for Rachel and Josh

THE TATTOOED MEN

PREFACE

IT IS NOT that the Japanese are so complex—it is that their complexities are different from ours. What makes everything more confusing is that at first glance they seem so much like us, and first-time visitors to Japan are often swept into something which is known in our family as the Pittsburgh Syndrome. The bustling cities, the booming factories, department stores, theaters, nightclubs, supermarkets and superhighways all remind us of the cities we've come from. Only the lettering on the billboards and signs is different, and we have the illusion that if we could only read them it would be just like back home.

To many of us this is a great disappointment. We have come to see the mysterious East and it turns out to be Pittsburgh.

This is a delusion, as any long-time foreign resident of Japan can tell you. The longer you stay, the less familiar it seems—and even if you work at learning enough of the language to get by, it will not help you to understand Japanese concepts which are based on a very different history, culture and tradition from our own, and which produce a kind of logic which is often totally unrelated to our own notions of what is "logical."

Nevertheless I had not anticipated any great "culture shock" in gathering the material for this book. I had already gone through that on my first visit to Japan, and though there had been a few minor tremors on each subsequent visit, I reasoned that I would be dealing with a subject which was capable of isolation from the rest of the society: crime. If anything, I told myself, there would probably be greater similarities between the *yakuza* of Japan and the mafia of the United States than between any two comparable segments of our respective societies. As I realized that the very nature of a criminal subculture isolates it from the society on which it preys, I felt that I could pluck out this one, little-known segment of life in Japan and perhaps illuminate it a bit without getting caught up in the complexities of the rest of the social structure.

It took no time at all for me to learn that I was as much a victim of the Pittsburgh Syndrome as all those tourists about whom I had been so patronizing, and that despite the fact that the Japanese criminal structure looks deceptively like our own, I was missing an essential point. The criminals are Japanese. As such, any attempt by a foreigner to separate them from the country of which they are a part or, in understanding them, to apply criteria which ignore the rest of Japan, is like trying to figure out a jigsaw puzzle by looking at one piece.

Thus I found myself reaching for help from anthropologists, sociologists, psychologists, historians and savants in many fields not directly related to crime. Naturally I spoke with law-enforcement people and many criminals (lower and upper echelon) as well, and to my happy surprise I found everyone to be most generous and forthcoming. I say "surprise," because I had been warned that information would be difficult to come by because, as one police official put it, "We Japanese have a tendency to sweep unpleasantness under a carpet."

I was never able to pin down the exact number of gangs which exist in Japan because the figure keeps changing from year to year, but all estimates were awesome, ranging from two thousand to five thousand. Most of the small gangs are affiliated with one another under the umbrella of one of the dozen major gangs around the country. I chose to focus most of my attention on the Yamaguchi-gumi because it is the biggest, and because it is led by the man considered to be the most powerful gangster in the country, truly a "godfather of godfathers." How the gang got that big and how he got that powerful were what interested me.

Among the sources I went to for this information, I should like especially to mention one which was totally unexpected; certain memoirs which I ran across in a magazine called *Asahi Geino,* which were dictated by the leader himself. As they were written in Japanese, a language which does not lend itself to word-for-word translation in a way that would make sense to an American, I worked with an interpreter to extract the essential spirit of such portions of his chronicles which I have included in this book. Where it was possible to quote him directly, of course I did so and have so indicated. With respect to that particular material, it would have been naive, of course, to accept his unsupported word (although he was surprisingly frank), but fortunately I had access to a less emotionally charged account of his career—a police report which goes into copious detail about the same events. And, of course, I spoke with dozens of people who knew and know him. By the time I actually met him myself, it was like meeting an old friend.

Long before I got to that point—before, in fact, I had even left for Japan—I found myself the grateful recipient of sound advice and concrete help from some very knowledgeable people, and I should like to acknowledge their invaluable assistance and heart-warming encouragement in a project about which I was very tentative in the beginning. Jim Greenfield, for example. He is the dynamic foreign editor of the *New York Times*, had spent many years in Tokyo, and when I told him what I had in mind, he sat me down in the *Times* newsroom and put their files at my disposal. After that, he alerted the Tokyo bureau and asked that they help me if I should call on them. (I did and they did, and I am now forever in debt to Mr. Richard Halloran and Mr. Ofusa of that bureau, who made my life much easier by digging out every scrap of material they had which might furnish me with clues.)

Mr. Greenfield's warm response took a lot of the tentativeness out of my thinking, as did that of Selig Harrison, who had been the Tokyo correspondent of the *Washington Post* for many years. We had become friends on a previous trip, and I wrote to him asking if he could point my nose in a helpful direction. He immediately sent me a file bulging with material he had accumulated over the years on the subject of crime in Japan. Both these men and a number of other journalists who had been posted in Japan at some point in their careers gave me the names of people to call upon, but at the outset I was reluctant to do this since I felt it was a little sticky to ask total strangers for help. Nevertheless I jotted down every name in my notebook, to be used, I told myself, only in case of emergency. I was determined not to become what I have heard Bernard Krisher, Tokyo bureau chief of *Newsweek,* refer to as a "parachute author"—somebody who drops in on a country, picks everyone's brains and rushes home to write a book. In no time at all I overcame this high-minded resolve and called everyone in the book, Bernie Krisher himself first of all. Clearly, as I now refer to him as Bernie, calling him turned out to be an excellent move. He was not only a mine of information—he was as patient and gentle an informant as ever got button-holed by a frantic brain-picker.

I am deeply beholden to all of these people, as I am to many old friends from previous trips who were helpful far beyond any call of friendship in shepherding, steering, digging and driving me all around the country to help me chase down material I was seeking. I should like to mention Jiro Tamiya and Kinya Kitaoji in particular, both first-rate actors who have coincidentally played many gangster roles in films, and who are more than casually conversant with the role of real-life gangsters in their profession; Bob Strickland, a one-man conglomerate with several businesses in Tokyo and a thriving restaurant in Kyoto whose many years as a businessman, former nightclub performer and resident of Japan have brought him into contact with gangsters at many levels; Arthur Miyazawa, a new friend who teaches at a university and conducts a thriving import-export business as well, and who lent me his expertise as a historian; Rene Mayer, another businessman and long-time resident of Japan, who brought me into contact with the business community; Miss Yoko Sakai, a very old friend who by the greatest good fortune works as an interpreter, and who is not only bilingual but bicultural. The translations she did for me were invaluable.

(Yoko-san was alternately fascinated and appalled by what she considered to be a very odd choice of subject. No well-bred Japanese lady would have had any truck with gangsters, and I had to keep assuring her that I was not endangering my life. I had the same problem with Tetsuko Kuroyanagi, whom I think of more as a daughter than a friend. Tetsuko-san is a very busy actress—a daily talk show on TV, a few shows in the evening, and roles in the theater when she can sandwich them in. In between, she drove me around and worried about me.)

However, it is S. Chang of *Time* magazine's Tokyo bureau to whom I owe my greatest debt of gratitude. He is the man to whom I wrote in the first place to explain what I had in mind, and who sent me a cable in reply which said, "Welcome to Japan. Will help you all I can." All he could was considerable, for without his help I could never have gotten to see some of the people who were most important to me. He is not, of course, responsible for my opinions or for the conclusions and editorializing I may have done along the way. I bear the full brunt of blame for these.

Florence Rome

Photographs follow pages 152 and 210.

CHAPTER 1

ONE OF THE best-kept secrets about Japan is the fact that the Japanese have a criminal underground society which is bigger than the mafia. I don't mean that it is a secret from the Japanese or that it is something which has been deliberately withheld from the rest of the world, but for a variety of reasons, it seems to have escaped the attention of the West. And yet, there it is, as big or bigger than life, carrying on in the fine old Chicago tradition of the '30s (with some Oriental variations and innovations), and it carries with it a full complement of the flamboyant antics of that period such as shoot-outs, godfathers, ritualistic ceremonies and private "codes of honor" which filled the pages of the newspapers in the bad old days of my youth.

Our public enemies, from Al Capone through Lucky Luciano to Carlo Gambino, have been headline fodder for the rest of the world, and our international notoriety as a crime-wracked country has certainly been helped along by the annual output of books and flicks which are bent on glorifying the American hoodlum. *The Untouchables* was a top-rated TV offering in Japan, and *The Godfather* was an SRO smash on the Ginza, and I can recommend a little speakeasy-type private club in Tokyo (at least it was there on my last visit) called The Al Capone for anyone genuinely nostalgic for those vintage years. It has a peephole, a placé for you to whisper "Joe sent me" or its Japanese equivalent, and the waiters are dressed in pinstriped suits with heavily padded shoulders and black slouch hats pulled down low on their foreheads. The mafia, it would appear, is one of our more successful cultural exports.

But have you ever heard of Kazuo Taoka, for example? Or Kakuji Inagawa, or perhaps Michio Sasaki? I didn't think so. And yet they are as powerful—in some ways even more so—than our local product, for the range of their activities not only includes the usual garden-variety gangster activities such as drugs, prostitution, smuggling, and gambling, but has affected such respectable facets of the Japanese society as big business and politics.

The Japanese gift for publicizing the beautiful and graceful aspects of life in their country is infinitely greater than our own, and most of the stories one reads on the subject of crime in their country have to do with the relative safety and absence of crime in the streets in Japanese cities. Comparative statistics are offered, one for example which pointed to the fact that three murders by handgun were committed in Tokyo during a period in which five hundred thirty-eight such murders were committed in New York. Somewhat enviously, I add my own praise for the security I have always felt strolling around the cities of Japan, and for the superb police work which has created this phenomenon. Nevertheless street crime and organized crime are two very different things.

Once in a while, if you search for them, you will find stories which deal with that other side. In *Newsweek* in 1971 there was one which started: "Like flower arranging and the tea ceremony, the *yakuza*, or gangster, is an enduring feature of Japanese life." Another appeared in *Time* in February 1973. It was written by S. Chang, a first-rate journalist in *Time*'s Tokyo bureau who had succeeded in gaining an exclusive interview with the number one gangster of Japan, the man who is known as the godfather of godfathers. This particular story had more than normal interest for me because Mr. Chang is a friend of mine—but regardless, it was an extraordinary story, speaking of hosts of gangsters which outnumber even our own, and opening a door on their extensive involvement in the day-to-day life of Japan.

I suppose the chief reason that Mr. Chang's story rang such a bell in my mind is that I already knew from personal experience that there were gangsters, mafia style, in Japan. I had no idea as to the size and extent of the organization, but I did know that it existed. In point of fact, I had actually been wined and dined by one of their number—not number one, to be sure, but someone with sufficient prestige in gangster circles so that if I had been aware at the time of who he was, I should certainly have been impressed. All I did know was that he was a lavish and generous host, full of little jokes and good humor. I had no reason to think he was anything other than a solid citizen, an impression which was enhanced by the fact that uncharacteristically for a Japanese, he had brought his wife and son with him to the party. Who would ever have dreamed that this affable family man had been responsible for putting out a seek-and-destroy contract on one friend of mine, and had given his consent that another friend be "taught a lesson" by having her throat cut up a bit!

If this sounds improbable, so was the whole reason for our being in Tokyo at the time. The year was 1969, and my husband and I had come to Japan for the production of a musical based on Margaret Mitchell's epic of the old South, *Gone With the Wind,* for which my husband had written the music and lyrics. The whole extraordinary project had been the brain child of the Toho Company, one of Japan's leading theatrical production companies. They were blazing a trail, for although they had successfully imported American musicals in the past, this would be the first to originate there, with a Japanese cast and in the Japanese language.

In a burst of eager-beaverism we applied ourselves to the task of learning a bit of the language before going to Japan. We were not so unrealistic as to tackle anything in depth, but we thought it would be nice if we knew enough to cope with cab drivers and waiters, exchange a few greetings, ask prices, comment on the weather and so forth.

The Japanese language seems deceptively easy in the beginning, and one is apt to be carried away by minor successes. By the time we arrived in Tokyo we were congratulating each other on such triumphant mastery of the tongue as being able to say, "I think it's going to rain." After a few days of living in a hotel where we were effectively insulated against anything having remotely to do with living in Japan, we decided to take the plunge and move into an apartment.

Since obviously we didn't know one neighborhood from another, we chose a flat in one of the livelier sections of a district called Shinjuku-ku. Now there *are* parts of Shinjuku which are respectably residential, but our neighborhood was wall-to-wall cafes, snack bars, clip joints and *pachinko* parlors. For the benefit of those who have never gotten calluses on their thumbs playing *pachinko,* these are the vertical pinball games which line both sides of four or five aisles in the establishments where the game is played. For one's skill in sending the steel balls into the proper slots, one is rewarded with gifts such as candy, cigarettes and cheap gewgaws. In addition to simple-minded suckers like me, *pachinko* parlors seem to attract quite a few low elements, hoods, toughs, small-time gangsters. Among such elements, then, was our little nest. It was situated in what Japanese hipsters call "Cockroach Alley," a colorful detail which the real-estate agent who found it for us neglected to mention. It was my friend—she of the slashed throat—who whooped with laughter when I told her where we were living and who proceeded to fill me in on my environment. Instead of being indignant, though, I was rather pleased with the whole idea and perhaps that says something about me.

But even though our neighborhood was colorful and somewhat bizarre, our flat was almost as exotic as a Holiday Inn. I wish it had also been as convenient and comfortable, for the truth is that I am a spoiled, middle-class woman who dotes on such things as central heating, drains that work and hot water—things which I would generally take for granted in a flat for which we were paying four hundred fifty dollars a month. Our two rather dreary rooms, abysmally furnished with plastic chairs and sofa, had no such luxuries, and I mention all this only to explain why my initial burst of enthusiasm for keeping house in Japan was spent overnight. Each morning, as soon as I had finished whatever household chores had to be done, I would flee the flat and rush to the more satisfying atmosphere of the Imperial Theater, where rehearsals of *Scarlett*, as the show was called in Japan, were in progress. It was during these rehearsals that I struck up a friendship with Tokiko-san, which by the way is not her name. She prefers not to be identified since, as she puts it, "What happened to me could not be helped, and besides, it is finished now. I had a small hurt, but it could have been a big hurt, so I was lucky. To make much of it now, maybe it would change the luck. If you use another name, it will be as if it happened to another person." Bad luck would have been if she had wound up at the bottom of Tokyo Bay in what used to be called a cement kimono in Chicago days.

Tokiko-san was—still is, I'm delighted to say—an absolute knockout, a bona fide ravishing beauty. It has been a lot of years since I hung up my eyelashes and retired from the competition, but even if I were her age, I'd think it over very carefully before I risked the erosion of my ego by walking down a street with her to invite comparison. The nice part of it was that Tokiko-san didn't take herself seriously as a capital-B beauty, but was instead a warm, giggly girl with whom it was great fun to trade theater customs and gossip about our respective countries. She was not a member of the cast of *Scarlett*, her milieu being nightclubs, where she was a pop singer with, I was told, a big following. Her frequent presence at rehearsals was accounted for by the fact that she was, well, Keeping Company we used to call it, with an important member of the Japanese production staff. (We had two staffs, ours and theirs.) While not a daily visitor as I was, she was around often enough for us to work up the kind of easy familiarity which is characteristic of theater people in every country I've ever been in, and sometimes, when we had both had enough of watching the director put the cast through their paces, we'd sneak out and go on minitours of the city in her tiny car.

Tokyo is a big sprawling place which has resisted all efforts at city planning. I have a private theory about that, which is that it has been razed to the ground so often, what with one thing and another such as earthquakes and bombs, that the city fathers haven't thought it worthwhile to roll up their sleeves to work out something permanent. Of course, there are other factors, such as that the urban population of Japan has increased so dynamically in so short a period of time that it would be impossible for any plans to keep up with the mushrooming growth. The result is a helter-skelter makeshift of a city in which even cab drivers cannot find their way around without maps and explicit directions. Tokiko-san, however, knows and delights in every irrational twist of her home town, and she had a missionary's zeal in opening it up to me. We went on treasure hunts through improbable alleys so that she could show me a special garden or shrine or house, and to tiny shops behind other tiny shops in quarters where foreigners were so rare a phenomenon that I sometimes felt like Admiral Perry. All the time she would keep up a running stream of chatter in her delightful Japlish, sometimes surprisingly raunchy for a nice Japanese girl, and sometimes filled with those exquisitely polite phrases.

It was from Tokiko-san that I used to learn slang words which astonished my more conservative Japanese friends. Occasionally she would caution me against the use of certain words in polite society, saying, "That is a gangster word. Don't use it when you are with nice people." (As a matter of fact, she taught me quite a lot about the special role of language in Japan, and the gradations of speech which tell a person who you are and where you belong on the social scale.) I learned from her the word for gangster—*yakuza* (pronounced YAHK-za), and I certainly saw nothing strange in the fact she knew so much of the special jargon of gangsters. After all, I'm fairly knowledgeable about gangster lingo in English, as is anyone who has ever read a book about gangsters or seen a '30s movie, and though I may have entertained a few fantasies on the subject when I was growing up in Chicago, I'm hardly a gangster's moll. Now, about her throat.

Tokiko-san always wore a scarf, which she draped over her hair and wound around her neck. It was pretty and colorful and I figured it was a protection for her hairdo and against the drafty rehearsal hall—a very sensible fashion accessory. One day, over tea, she asked me about the progress I was making with a book I had contracted to write which had to do with staging a musical in Japan. I told her that I hadn't really started writing it, that I was simply collecting information and making notes. She nodded thoughtfully and looked undecided, as though she were debating something she would like to say but wasn't entirely sure whether she ought to. Finally she drew a breath and blurted out, "I think maybe you should say something in your book about the *yakuza.*"

I raised an eyebrow. "The *yakuza?*" I said. "Why would I do that? They don't seem to have much to do with the story of Rhett and Scarlett and Melanie and Ashley in Japanese!"

"No, of course not," she said, "but they have much to do with the entertainment business in Japan, and maybe you should talk about it. You know Ashley? [She meant the actor who was playing Ashley, of course.] He can tell you some stories of *yakuza.* I too." As she spoke, she started to unwind her scarf, and when she had removed it, she pointed to her neck. "You see?" she said, and I found myself staring open-mouthed at a long, healed-over but still frightening scar which began just under her left ear and continued laterally to the middle of her neck. "I got it from *yakuza,*" she said, and as she caught the horrified expression on my face she laughed and added, "Nothing to worry about now, Florence-san. It's over, finished, and it could have been much worse. This was a warning so I should behave myself."

Her misbehavior had consisted of trying to fire her manager. As she described the incident, I had a sense

of *déjà vu,* that I had been there before. I had, too, for
Tokiko-san's tale bore a strong resemblance to the Joe
E. Lewis story, a gangster episode which made headlines in my Chicago days. Lewis, the great nightclub
comic, had been packing them in nightly at a place
called the Green Mill Garden back in 1927. It was the
time when illegal booze was a staple liquid refreshment
in such places, and even the most naive customers knew
that they were run by the Syndicate, one of those eu-
phemisms for the mafia. Nobody minded particularly.
Certainly not the entertainers who were well paid, the
customers who were well oiled, or the police who were
well greased. Lewis had many buddies among the hard-
eyed men with shoulder holsters—a breed which seems
always to have a soft spot for entertainers—but he made
the mistake of thinking that they would allow sentiment
to interfere with business. He announced to his boss
one day that he had accepted a better offer from a spot
called The Rendezvous, run by a rival mob, and he
shook his head at all efforts to dissuade him from making the change. A week later, after he had opened in his
new club, he was found in his dressing room with a
fractured skull, and with his throat and tongue slashed.
He recovered, after a fashion, with his speech permanently impaired, but his assailants were never punished
since Lewis claimed he could not recognize them. In the
texture of those violent times, it was probably a wise
decision on his part to keep his mouth shut.

As Tokiko-san rewound her scarf, she taught me
some of the facts of life which govern the entertainment
business in Japan. Very often, she said, entertainers
were allied with gangster-managers because of the stiff
competition, particularly among singers, and even

more particularly among female singers. For all of its frenzied entry into the twentieth century, Japan has not gone so far as to allow much change in the traditional role of women, certainly not to an extent which would impress Westerners. It *is* happening a little, but on the whole there are not many areas which offer a comparatively free life-style to women, and there is a reluctance to let them out of the psychological kimonos in which they have been wrapped for centuries. One area where escape is possible is entertainment, and it seemed to me when I was there that practically every pretty girl who can carry a tune dreams of a career in show business. Part of the lure is the same as it is everywhere else— money and glamor. The added factor in Japan is liberation of a sort, sometimes from family and tradition. Very often show business offers an escape from a kind of social discrimination as well. Whatever the reasons for wanting to be in show business, it is not unusual for an eager young performer to make a deal with a *yakuza* manager who promises her a short cut to fame and fortune. It is even possible for him to deliver on these promises, thanks to conditions all the way down the line: gangster-manager plus gangster-controlled nightclub or theater or motion picture studio equals job for aspiring performer.

Tokiko-san had made her deal early on in her career, but then she had begun to regret it. In a rash moment, she decided to have a frank talk with her manager, telling him she was not satisfied with the type of bookings he had been getting her, and that she felt she was entitled to sing in more prestigious clubs, where he apparently had no connections. She was sure he would understand, and goodbye, and can't we be friends and all that. He did his best to persuade her to reconsider, but when she seemed adamant, he bowed politely, left, and she breathed a sigh of relief, thinking the matter was settled. Only one thing nagged at her. She knew she should have discussed this first with a rather powerful "connection" she had and should have sought his advice on how to go about it, but since it had all ended amiably she was sure it was all right. She would explain it to him eventually, and if her erstwhile manager should by any chance decide to make a little trouble, she was certain her connection would go to bat for her.

Ten days later she opened her door to two thugs, emissaries from her former manager they told her, who also spoke politely and tried again to persuade her to change her mind. "I became nervous," she said, "and did the wrong thing. I ordered them to leave." Whereupon one of them seized and held her arms behind her back while the other produced a mean-looking knife, with which he inflicted the wound she had shown me— not deep enough to endanger her life, just a reminder of what she might have to expect if she were to go through with her plan.

As to her powerful connection, she was right to have worried about taking matters into her own hands without prior consultation with him, for in ignoring him she had herself set up a chain of seemingly inevitable actions. Her assailants had been petty thugs who had nothing against her personally, but who were under orders from their boss. Their boss was her manager, himself a small-time *yakuza* who was answerable to his *oyabun*.

"*Oyabun?*" I asked.

"*Oyabun,*" she said, "is the boss of the territory. It is

a word that means something like parent, only not a real parent, of course. Just the top man in the gang." (I checked later and found that it means literally "parent role," and that the members of the gang are called *kobun*, which means "child role.") Well, I wanted to know, what did this particular *oyabun* have against her? Nothing, she told me, except that she should have consulted him first, as he was the connection of whom she had spoken. "He is my father's friend, you see," she said. "My father owns a restaurant in the *nawabari* (territory) of this *oyabun*. I have known him a long time, and he was good to me and helped me in my career. He even picked my manager for me, so you see I hurt his 'face' by firing my manager without telling him. If he does not act to punish me, he will lose the respect of his *kobun*." Everybody was just doing his job, all the way down the line.

All clear? It was clear to me because I had long since stopped making snide little jokes about the grave importance of "face" to a Japanese. At that particular time, the Americans connected with *Scarlett* were living in a world of frustration produced by the elaborate intricacies of "face." Everything was taking twice as long as it had to because we were impatient to get on with the job. This impatience sometimes caused a Japanese counterpart to lose "face," and the result was that endless hours were needed to straighten things out.

"I should have remembered," Tokiko-san continued, "that *oyabun* had *giri* toward my manager." (*Giri* is duty, obligation based on relationship.) She sighed. "I know this is complicated for a foreigner to understand, but this is the Japanese way." I asked what the eventual result had been, and she said with a sunny smile, "Everything is okay now! We are all friends again. Everything is forgotten." Except for that scratch on the neck.

In spite of what she had told me, I had the feeling that hers must have been a rather special and isolated case, or if not precisely that, something which might happen only in the spicier areas of the entertainment business. There's a lot of snobbism in that world, and the theater is the *grande dame,* so to speak, on the most elevated rung of the social ladder. Nightclubs—well, yes, I was willing to accept that there could be gangsters involved in that sort of thing, but under no circumstances could I imagine them invading the sacred precincts of the Imperial Theater. Just the same, I thought I ought to follow through on Tokiko-san's suggestion that I speak to the actor who was playing Ashley.

His name is Jiro Tamiya, and that *is* his real name, and he is a star, an extraordinarily handsome and gifted one. Rehearsing his role as Ashley Wilkes, he was becoming each day more and more the very model of a high-born Southern patriot. I had been enormously impressed with his intelligent grasp of the Hamlet-like character, the indecisive well-beloved of Scarlett O'Hara—a role very far removed from the kind for which he had become famous in Japan—*yakuza* roles in pictures. In addition, his real-life manner is the elegant and polished behavior of a well-brought-up, well-educated man, and it was unthinkable to imagine him being in danger of losing his life because of some involvement with real-life *yakuza.* The fact was that the same kindly patron of the arts who had been responsible for Tokiko's problems had only recently rescinded the contract on Tamiya-san's life.

I already had a lot of rapport with Tamiya-san, partly

because his English was a lot better than that of most of the other members of the company, and he was always anxious to improve it, so we often chatted and my instructions from him were to correct his mistakes. He did the same for me with my primitive Japanese, but I hardly felt that this was sufficient basis for me to jump in flat-footed with a question like "Tell me, Jiro-san, how'd you get yourself mixed up with gangsters?" I thought of various approaches and I finally decided on "Tell me, Jiro-san, how'd you get yourself mixed up with gangsters?" To my relief he laughed.

"Before I answer that," he said, "ask me how I got mixed up with show business."

"All right," I said, "how'd you get mixed up in show business?"

"Ah," he said. "Well, about show business, would you believe I won a Mr. Japan contest?" I certainly would believe it, but I wondered why he had entered such a contest to begin with.

"I entered on a dare when I was in college," he said, "and when I won I had to decide whether to quit school. My ambition had been to be a lawyer, but then all of a sudden I had a picture in my mind of a different kind of life." While he was debating what to do, he was approached by a major film studio, Toei, which as it happens specializes in gangster films, the only ones which make any real money in Japan. That settled it. It sounded more glamorous than the law, and he opted to give it a whirl. If it didn't work out he could always go back to school.

He kept whirling at Toei for fourteen years, onward and upward in bigger and better roles until he had become a very valuable property from the studio's

point of view. Moreover, he had established an unusu-
ally close relationship with the studio head. "We were,"
he said, "like father and son. Have you ever heard the
expression *oyabun-kobun?*"

"Oh yes," I said, quite pleased with myself, "gangster
talk."

He was shocked. "Oh *no,*" he said, "not just gangster
talk. This kind of relationship is everywhere. Boss to
employee, teacher to student, senior person to junior
person everywhere. Always there is an *oyabun* and
kobun."

At any rate, as it must for all actors, the day arrived
when Tamiya-san found himself in a hassle about bill-
ing. He was being costarred in a film, and he felt that
he had seniority over his costar and that his name
should come first. The producer of the film—not his
oyabun—had decided otherwise, and Tamiya-san, outraged that his seniority was being disregarded, felt that
he had no other course open to him but to leave Toei.
"You understand, Florence," he said, "it was a matter
of 'face.'" I nodded. He went on to say that in deference to his *oyabun* he had gone to see him to explain the
circumstances and to announce that at the termination
of his contract with the studio he would leave.

Well sir, affectionate relationship or no, his *oyabun*
fixed him with that same fishy stare which I understand
the late M-G-M chief Louis B. Mayer used to turn on
actors who got balky, and he treated him to a long
lecture on the subject of all the studio had done for him,
throwing in a few thousand words on the subject of *giri*
for good measure. Tamiya-san didn't argue any of the
points and he listened politely and attentively to everything his *oyabun* had to say. But, as he would be the first

to admit, he's a stubborn cuss. He falls into no meek, submissive Japanese stereotype image. On the contrary, he is something which is called an *ippiki-okami,* a lone wolf, which is not a status which wins popularity contests in Japan, where one is expected to fit into the group ethic and not go off on one's own. I find this characteristic to be one of the great differences in our national personalities, for while we Americans publicly profess to admire gutsy and independent behavior for the purpose of improving our lot, the Japanese prefer people who don't make waves which upset the status quo, even when they have a right to do so. Tamiya-san, feeling totally justified in his position, listened quietly to his *oyabun* and when he had finished making his case, the actor told him with the deepest personal regret that with all due respect, he was leaving as soon as his contract was up.

Now it's a funny thing about those studio contracts in Japan. They work only one way. Renewal on the part of the actor is automatic and expected—provided the studio wants him—and the five or six major studios have an agreement to blacklist any actor who tries to move out of his home studio without permission, even if his legal obligation no longer exists. Tamiya-san knew all about that, and he also knew some of the dramatic consequences suffered by actors who had tried to buck the system. He had several sleepless nights anticipating what could happen to him, thinking about people like Kazuo Hasegawa, for instance. This was an actor even more renowned than he, who had worked for Toei for thirty years, and whose knife-scarred face was a memento of a decision to strike out on his own. And there was Fujiko Yamamoto, a great actress who

had made a similar decision and who had become instantly unemployable in spite of her reputation all over
Japan. No scars, but no jobs either since that time. The
profit that was to be made on her was obviously not so
important as the example which had to be set. Yes, and
there were scores of others for him to think about as he
tossed in bed, but still—the matter of "face" was un-
resolved and Tamiya-san felt he had to risk it. Besides,
hope springeth eternally, etc., and he nurtured a slim
hope that perhaps his *oyabun* would simmer down after
a while and find it in his heart to understand and to
forgive.

This unwarranted optimism went out the window
one night when he left his house and a black limousine
without headlights tried to run him down. Love him like
a son, he might, but the boss was not about to overlook
a major piece of insubordination. If Tamiya-san were to
succeed in his defiance of the system, it could give rise
to all sorts of frightening possibilities: the establishment of something socialistic like the Screen Actors'
Guild, or an Actors' Equity, for instance. To nip such
a possibility in the bud, Tamiya's case was put into the
hands of the experts who looked after Toei's best interests, and a couple of hit men were assigned the job of
making him permanently unemployable.

He got the message and lost no time in hustling his
wife and family out of Tokyo, after which he proceeded
to live in what was virtually a fortress. Shades were
drawn, doors were locked, and he ventured out only in
broad daylight to knock at TV studio doors, stage
doors, other film studio doors, none of which would
open to him. The word had gone out that Jiro Tamiya
was poison, was probably not long for this world, and

that anyone who employed him would find himself in the same fix. He was scared, but he felt no rancor for he had known the rules, assessed the possibilities, and the decision to buck the tide and risk the result had been his own.

Salvation on one front appeared in the unlikely person of another *yakuza* boss, who was a movie buff and an ardent fan of Tamiya-san. Not surprisingly, the *yakuza* are among the most devoted admirers of *yakuza* films, which furnish them with historical justification for their lives, and which portray them as romantic and virile specimens. Sometimes they make strong identification with the actors who play in them, men like Jiro Tamiya and Ken Takakura. Jiro has told me that in public places the gangsters sometimes confuse him with the real thing, treating him like a blood brother, sitting down in restaurants with him, insisting on buying him drinks. In any case, Tamiya-san's savior was semi-retired, having become involved in many legitimate businesses, but he still knew his way around very well and he wanted to do a good deed for his hero.

He invited him down to his headquarters and talked to him like a benevolent father. He had already rounded up two of his own toughest *kobun*, who were to act as bodyguards for Tamiya-san, and then he made a few phone calls to pave the way for a meeting between hunted and nemesis, advising him to beard the lion in his den, with the bodyguards behind him, of course. He also coached him in exactly what he was to say, and Tamiya-san followed his instructions to the letter. A great deal of face-saving ritual was necessary but the presence of the bodyguards was just as important, for it showed that now Tamiya-san had some powerful backing of his own. The affair was concluded and his life was no longer an issue.

His career, however, was and probably would have remained so, had it not been for the fact that my husband and the director of *Scarlett* thought he would be ideal for the role of Ashley. None of us in the American group knew anything about Tamiya-san's problems, but the Toho Company did, and in view of our desire to cast him they took a hand. I have been told that their creative head, Kazuo Kikuta (who has since died), spoke to the right people, and while I have no way of knowing this for certain, it seems likely to me that he pointed out the international nature of the project and made it a patriotic issue! In any case, Tamiya-san was free to go back to work and he has been doing so very successfully ever since. I suppose this accounts in part, at least, for the warmth we felt from him from the moment we met.

The punishing *oyabun* who figured in both these incidents is someone whom I must call Mr. H. at the request of both Tamiya-san and Tokiko-san. It is not a fear of reprisal that engendered the request, but in the case of Tokiko-san he is, as she explained, a friend of her father and now once again her friend. As for Tamiya-san, he says, "You see he has many other businesses which have nothing to do with being a *yakuza*. Besides he is getting old and would like to be thought of as respectable. You would be surprised how much he does for charity and the kind things he does for people. We have become friends and I really like him."

It was only after we had returned to the United States that I learned that this same Mr. Nice Guy had been our host at dinner one night in one of Tokyo's most elegant (and expensive, whew!) restaurants. The invitation had come to us through one of the dozens of semiofficial people who were always hanging around rehearsals. The Toho Company is the artistic branch of a conglomerate which owns department stores, railroads and various other enterprises. This branch has motion picture producing companies, theaters, a form of Kabuki, Takarazuka, nightclubs, and this special section devoted to the production of Western-style theater, so I always assumed that all those people whom I couldn't identify were connected with one or another of the Toho departments which were consumed with curiosity to see how the American production staff went about doing their jobs. This was a learning experience as well as a profit-making enterprise for them (for us too), for if there is one branch of theater in which we do seem to have the edge on most countries, it is in the production of musicals. Mr. H. was there frequently, chatting amiably with kibitzers and with various members of the staff and the cast, and I was told by an intermediary that he wished to make a gesture to show his appreciation to so many "great talents" (his words, not mine) who had come from the United States for this unique project. Flattery always gets you somewhere so naturally we accepted.

I was seated at the right of Mr. H., and we hit it off cozily despite a few communication problems. My earnest attempts to make conversation in Japanese were matched by his in English, so with wigwags, gestures and a few bilingual members of the party to jump into the breach when necessary, we managed. I asked him what his position was in the Toho organization, and he waved his hand back and forth in front of his face in that frantic gesture which always makes Americans think they've said something frightfully gauche, but which actually means just plain "no," with varying degrees of vehemence, depending on how agitated the gesture becomes. "I'm not connected with Toho," he said, "except in an informal way when I can help with a problem. I love theater and try to do what I can."

With a flourish he extracted a card from his case and presented it to me. It said that he is a business consultant, president of a firm, all very neat and legitimate-looking with a cable address and that sort of thing. I later learned that he is indeed a man to consult if you don't want to have labor problems, or accidents to personnel and equipment at your place of business, or if you are in need of raising money to finance an enterprise which banks have already turned down as being too risky. Mr. H. is reputed to be very good at solving such problems, and it is rumored that he has an even greater talent for creating problems which require his services to solve. But never mind, he was an easy laugher with an impressive array of gold teeth, and all right, I liked him very much. I could cover myself on this point by observing that I didn't know who he was, but the chances are I would have liked him anyway. As Tamiya-san had told me, he's a very nice man. It's too bad but there you are: villains and rascals are very often more attractive and more fun than the good guys.

Looking back, it's only natural that I should have learned of the existence of the *yakuza* from entertainers. The two worlds have many of the same attractions—money, excitement, glamor—and while such considerations are tempting even if you don't happen to come out of a background of poverty and/or discrimination, the fact remains that a disproportionate number of people in the entertainment world and in the gangs do spring from such roots. For a lot of them, the paths they chose represented the only way they could lay their hands on some of the world's goods, but whatever the reasons, they understand one another's needs and hang-ups and problems, and an empathy exists between them, based on a shared background.

While I am speaking principally of Japan, it has been true in this country too, more so in the past, but it still exists to an extent. Gangsters and performers sharing nightclub tables are not an uncommon sight and there have been scandals involving stars and their mafia connections. Nor was it too long ago that the "respectable" community considered "actress" and "whore" to be synonymous, as were "actor" and "thief." Generally speaking, players were not people who were allowed in the front door. These days, however, we do find the society columns studded with names of glittering performers who are allowed to mix with the quality folk, but in Japan show-biz people are for the most part still in the social doghouse. There are a few exceptions, of course, but the point is that they *are* exceptions. Their resulting self-consciousness makes them a lot more comfortable with one another—and sometimes with *yakuza*—than with "civilians."

This social discrimination comes to full flower when the artists happen to be *konketsu*, people of mixed blood, which as it happens a great many of them are, with the mixture generally being Korean or Chinese with Japanese, but there are also some reminders of the GI occupation, both white and black. I recall having been struck with the beauty and talent of a Takarazuka actress (Takarazuka being the all-female theater—the answer to the all-male Kabuki) and commenting about her to some non-show-business Japanese friends. The invariable reply was a variation of "Oh yes, I have seen her. You know of course that she is half Korean." Not a word about her looks or her talent.

The ties between entertainers and gangsters have unfortunately been known to go beyond mere empathy and *camaraderie,* or even beyond the gangster-actor managerial relationship. An actor named Isihara was picked up for smuggling guns for some of his friends, and another *cause célèbre* was Ando, a popular singer-actor and part-time *yakuza* who was convicted of murder. There has been an assortment of celebrities who have been hauled into court for pushing drugs to colleagues at the behest of gangster pals. About Ando, incidentally, it is said that after he had served his term he gave up his gangster connections and is back in show business full time. In addition to acting, he does some technical consultation on *yakuza* films. Naturally.

Well anyway, my interest in the *yakuza* world began with show business, and all these memories flooded back to me in New York when I read Mr. Chang's article in *Time* four years later. His piece also made me realize that if the figure quoted—one hundred fifty thousand gangsters—was correct, they must certainly be involved in a lot more than show business. So how come nobody with whom I had spoken had ever heard of them? Travelers—that is to say, shrine-hoppers, flower-arrangement fans, and the like—looked blank when I mentioned them. There were a few old Asia hands who had lived and worked there who did know about the *yakuza* and who nodded grimly when I spoke of them, after which they advised me to stay away, they were an ugly lot, and if I wanted to write a book why didn't I stick to the beauties of Mount Fuji or geisha girls.

The subject kept nagging at me, however, even though I discussed it with an assortment of loved ones, dear old friends who felt it their duty to be absolutely honest with me by telling me I was off my rocker. They pointed out with all the best intentions in the world, I'm *sure*, that I am, after all, a woman within whistling distance of Social Security. They mentioned in passing that the amount of Japanese I had picked up was not enough to qualify me to conduct any interviews. They let it drop that even if I could speak Japanese, what made me think that any gangsters would be moved to tell me the story of their lives? Against that sort of "encouragement," I balanced Jim Greenfield et al., and then I packed, said goodbye to the ones I was still speaking to, and left.

CHAPTER 2

A WONDERFUL kickoff, I had
thought, would be to meet the Mr. Big about whom Mr.
Chang had written. It seemed a logical place to begin,
and I am embarrassed to remember that I thought it
would be a cinch. I had the best of auspices—Mr. Chang
himself—and all it would take would be a phone call to
set up a date. I was, in fact, quite surprised that other
friends to whom I mentioned my plan, a few experienced journalists among them, seemed to feel that
it would not be all that easy. The godfather had been
a sick man, they told me, and he stuck very close to his
hearth; he saw only trusted friends and colleagues; he

was known to be very suspicious of foreigners generally, and, uh, a foreign *woman* was not exactly an ideal
status, if I saw what they meant. When I reported all
these things to Mr. Chang, he merely smiled and said,
"We'll see." If he had said, "That's nonsense!" or
words to that effect I would have felt better, but "We'll
see" gave me misgivings. I went from "cinch" to "it's
impossible" in my own mind overnight.

Mr. Chang shares with me a love of challenges, but
if I had known then how much wheeling and dealing it
was going to take, I don't think I would have had the
nerve to ask him to arrange this meeting. Fortunately
I didn't know—in the beginning, that is. I began to get
the idea when he called me from time to time to make
progress reports, and my guilt at putting him to all this
trouble became so great that I had just about reached
the point of saying, "Look, forget it, thank you for
trying," when he called and said, "It's all set."

What that meant was that the machinery was in motion. There were still ploys and counterploys which had
to be made, and I began to have the illusion that I was
part of a cops-and-robbers charade. It was an illusion
which disappeared only when our car drove up to the
house on the outskirts of Kobe where the meeting was
to take place, for this was certainly no movie set. It was
very real—concrete and wood, firmly implanted by the
side of the road. I had pictured it in my mind as palatial.
It wasn't that, but it was certainly large and imposing by
Japanese standards, partially obscured from the road by
lush shrubbery, and separated from its neighbors by a
high wrought-iron fence and by heavily bolted gates.

Nor had the four muscular, expressionless men
standing behind those gates been sent over by Central

Casting. They were the McCoy, genuine gangsters awaiting our arrival with their arms folded across their chests, dressed identically in T-shirts, fawn-colored slacks and house slippers. They wore sunglasses and their hair was crew-cut in approved *yakuza* fashion. The Palace Guard, I thought, and indeed considering all the ingenuity Mr. Chang had employed to get me here, this could not have been more complicated if I had sought an audience with the Emperor. But after all, why not? The occupant of this well-guarded house represented a pinnacle of power in his special world as total and as unchallenged as that of His Imperial Highness.

His name is Kazuo Taoka, and it is a name known to everyone but the most sheltered recluse in the country. Some speak of him with loathing, some with considerable affection and deep regard, but even those who loathe him speak of him with respect. If there is such a thing as an *oyabun no oyabun,* a godfather of godfathers, Kazuo Taoka is it, for he is the head of the Yamaguchi-gumi, the largest and most powerful criminal syndicate in Japan, about which there is a popular saying that "even a crying child becomes quiet when he hears the name Yamaguchi-gumi." He is the absolute monarch of the ten thousand men who are directly affiliated with his organization in a network of gangs which cover the Kansai, or western part of the country, but his influence extends into the Kanto, or eastern area of the country, which includes Tokyo, and his quiet boast is that ten thousand (which is the police estimate) is the tenth part of the number of men over whom he has control. Together with the other gangs of Japan, this is the mafia, the formidable army of *yakuza.*

Unlike the Emperor's, the mantle worn by Kazuo

Taoka was not handed down to him in a direct line of succession from the Sun Goddess. He has earned it. He has fought for it with his own two hands, using the tools of violence and murder when they were called for—but it was not these alone which have put him where he is, for these are tools which all *yakuza* know how to use. Kazuo Taoka's extra added ingredient is a quality rare not only among *yakuza*, but among most men—a stunning and unique intelligence. Plus one other thing, which wins the admiration of even his most vocal enemies, the police—a tremendous gift for personal public relations.

For example, in that *Time* story, Mr. Chang had etched out a portrait of a man which resembled no gangster I had ever heard of. He had emerged from his interview as part statesman, part patriot, part benefactor and part stand-up comic. ("Where do you get the money to pay for all these luxuries?" Mr. Chang had asked, to which Taoka had replied, "My wife saves it out of her housekeeping allowance." You bet. A few yen here, a few there, and next thing you know there's that chauffeur-driven car we had just arrived in. Pretty creative bookkeeping, that.) In his role as humanitarian, he had spoken with solemnity of social ills and misfits, of discrimination, of society's responsibilities and failures. I'd read interviews with Joe Columbo and other mafia capos which were full of self-justification and screams of persecution, but I never had read anything that matched Taoka's statement: "What I need," he had said, "is the services of some scholars in finding ways and means of securing mental and spiritual relief for my membership. So many of them were born emotionally insecure." And naturally he had insisted that the

Yamaguchi-gumi is not a criminal society at all. Simply a mutual-aid, self-help brotherhood under his concerned guidance. When I read it I remember thinking, *who does he think he's kidding?* As I boarded my plane a few months later to try to meet this extraordinary man, echo had answered *you.*

And here I was, standing in his front hall, being helped out of my shoes and into slippers, which are provided for guests in Japanese households. On the trip to his house the thought crossed my mind—just crossed, it didn't really take root—that a man who held such total control over the lives of so many thousands of men might not be too amiably disposed toward a nosy woman prying into his life. I didn't expect him to poison my tea, but I was very sensitive about the impression I might make, not so much for my own sake, but because of the deep obligation I felt to Mr. Chang. He was also being helped into his slippers, having come along to buoy me up, to introduce me, to keep me from putting my big American foot in my mouth, and to translate. My concern centered on the fact that I did not wish to jeopardize Mr. Chang's standing in this household which, since he was a journalist with an inside track, was certainly important to him. This made me nervous, but I was also quite depressed for a different reason, which was that I had been put into a verbal strait-jacket. I had been told in no uncertain terms that I would have to comply with certain conditions before I would be allowed to talk with the great man about matters any weightier than the weather.

The bearer of these tidings had been Taoka's son, Mitsuru Taoka, and I'll get around to him and his conditions presently. At the moment, all I knew was that I'd come one hell of a long way to discuss barometric pressure with Japan's leading gangster, that my tape recorder, camera and notebook were *verboten*, and that my feet hurt.

We had started out, Mr. Chang and I, at eight o'clock that morning—a sweltering August Sunday morning—from Tokyo. Like New York, Tokyo is a summer festering of smog, heat and humidity, and this day had started out so piercingly hot that had there been no reason to do otherwise, I should not have budged from the air-conditioned comfort of my room. As it was, we had traveled by car to the Tokyo airport, by plane to Osaka, by bus to Kobe, and back to car again in order to get to the outskirts of town where Taoka lived. Now, at two o'clock in the afternoon with the sun at its most punishing, I felt as though I had run all the way. Actually I *had* done quite a lot of running, making connections from one form of transportation to another trying to keep up with Mr. Chang, who seemed maddeningly oblivious to such things as heat and fatigue. I was flattered that he treated me as a contemporary, capable of the same output of energy and stamina as he is, but the truth is that I outrank him by a lot of years for a starter, and I was adding a few more every minute. I would certainly not have complained even if I had felt like it, for in addition to everything else, I was beholden to Mr. Chang for having taken one of his few days of relaxation in his demanding schedule to do this very great service for me.

En route, I caught a glimpse of myself in a full-length mirror at the airport, and I'd like to buy back that look. Rivulets of moisture—no, let's be honest—of sweat were coursing through my makeup, my hairdo had gone limp, my white slack suit, so pristine, so crisp when I had started out, was a mess, and my feet were swollen out of sandals I should have had better sense than to wear. And of course, I was toting that piece of equipment which is standard for Americans abroad, an outsized shoulder bag with my personal and professional gear, the aforementioned tape recorder, etc., now just a lot of dead weight. I had worked so hard on the image I thought would be *de rigueur* for meeting gangsters—urbane, poised, worldly. What I saw in the mirror during that moment of truth was the real me, bedraggled, bothered and bewildered. *They were right,* I acknowledged to myself about all those warnings from friends, *you're not as young as you used to be.*

Our first stop when we arrived in Kobe was the Oriental Hotel, a name more titillating than descriptive. Thanks to all those scientific advances such as travel and communications which make for energy crises, most countries are managing to bury their national flavor under a decor which can only be described as International Rest Room Moderne. The Oriental Hotel in Kobe would not be out of place in Dubuque, Iowa, and stopping there had been the suggestion of Mitsuru Taoka, who was to meet us for luncheon and to give me my premeeting briefing before we trundled off on the last leg of our journey to meet his father.

Mitsuru-san and I greeted each other as old buddies, since this was not our first meeting. That one had taken place the previous Sunday at the Palace Hotel in Tokyo, also at a luncheon. Again this meeting was something which had been arranged by Mr. Chang, who had explained to me that I must first pass muster with Junior, because he was very protective of his father. As a parent

I considered that a laudable attitude, and I was predisposed to like him. Besides, I was curious to see what the second generation had turned out to be. I wondered whether he would be a chip off the old block, or whether like the sons of so many prominent men, he would have suffered from growing up in his father's shadow.

No way. The cocky, self-assured young man who strode forth to meet me in the lobby of the Palace was suffering from no psychological hang-ups which were immediately discernible to the eye. His father might be the number one gangster in Japan, but he had obviously behaved toward his son the way Jewish mothers are supposed to—providing him with advantages and opportunities which he himself had never had.

Mitsuru-san is, in fact, a product of Keio University, an institution of learning which reeks of prestige and privilege, one of the major universities which supply most of the great corporations of Japan with their executive personnel. He does not work for any of these, although he did for a few years after graduation put in time in the warehouse division of Mitsubishi. Neither is he a member of his father's corporation, the Yamaguchi-gumi. He is a theatrical agent and producer, president of his own firm, and I suppose it should be noted in passing that his father's connections have done him no harm in his profession, for Dad is not without influence in those circles. Nepotism is not, after all, the exclusive right of the legitimate society.

It's only a guess, but I would think that Mitsuru-san was pretty curious about me too. It was hard to tell since he was hidden behind dark sunglasses which covered half his face. Under the glasses were round young

cheeks and a winning smile, and beneath that was a
rather stocky torso covered in a hand-tailored maroon-
red suit, a blending shocking-pink shirt and a tie striped
in both colors. In contrast to the sober-suited, dark-tied
Japanese gentlemen with whom the dining room was
filled, Mitsuru-san looked like a peacock among pigeons. In case he didn't notice what I was wearing and
would like to note it in *his* memoirs, I was dressed in a
navy-and-white polka-dot dress, white shoes and even
gloves. I had worked out this costume along Stanis-
lavsky Method lines, the idea being to communicate
instantly that I was sober-minded, perfectly reliable and
not in the least occupied with sensationalism, an image
which I felt would make a twenty-nine-year-old boy who
might be a little sensitive about his father's occupation
feel more comfortable. As it turned out, he couldn't
have been more at ease, whereas my heart was zipping
along like a revved-up motor for fear that I would do
the wrong thing and blow the entire project. The only
indication he gave that having lunch with a *gaijin* (foreigner) who had traveled eight thousand miles to meet
his father was not necessarily routine was the fact that
his fingers kept drumming lightly and incessantly on
the table. He could have been just bored and restless,
I suppose, but I prefer not to think so.

In advance of the luncheon, I had mentioned to Mr.
Chang my regret at not knowing enough Japanese to
have an easy, normal conversation with Mitsuru-san.

"On the contrary," he said, "he will be a lot more
relaxed because you don't understand him, and freer to
say anything he likes to me." As it turned out, that
worked both ways, for Mr. Chang would advise me
quite openly on what line of questioning I ought to

pursue and counsel me on what answers I ought to give to Mitsuru-san's questions. I realize that this makes me sound a bit simple-minded, but our experience with *Scarlett* had taught me that there are certain techniques in talking with a Japanese which, unless they are observed, can lead to grave misunderstandings. My most valuable lesson at that time had come from Mr. Chang himself.

"We do not," he had said, "consider it necessarily a virtue to say everything that is on one's mind. Very often it is better to hold in reserve what might offend the listener." I had never forgotten it.

Actually I was surprised and a little pleased with myself at how much I *did* understand. Mitsuru-san seldom looked directly at me, since he was directing all of his conversation to Mr. Chang, and occasionally I had to bite my lip to keep from answering him directly instead of waiting for Mr. Chang to translate. "Why do you want to meet my father?" he said to Mr. Chang, who had already met his father, so I had to figure he meant me. I waited patiently for the translation and then delivered my prepared answer since I had been sure he would want to know that. I made a short speech which was filled with words like "charisma," and commented that no book dealing with *yakuza* would be complete without including the story of the number one *yakuza* in Japan. (I'd give a lot to know how Mr. Chang dealt with that word "charisma." I asked him but he wouldn't tell me. It must have had sexy overtones, judging from the quality of Mitsuru-san's laugh.)

In reply he made what sounded like an often-repeated speech of his own: "My father," he said, "is a great man. I would think that even if he were not my father. Perhaps being an American you cannot really understand what is meant by *yakuza*. You translate that as *gangster*, and so, of course, your mind immediately goes to the mafia in America which concerns itself only with crime and money. Our *yakuza* have an honorable tradition and a history of helping people. My father's whole life is based on what he can do for others."

As an old advertising woman, I recognize an excellent piece of hard sell when I hear it delivered by a sincere, convincing announcer. Besides it was rather refreshing to hear a boy speak so well of his parent in these liberated days and I told him that. I also told him something which had occurred to me about his father: that with a few alterations in his background, from all I knew of him, Taoka senior has all the gifts which would qualify him to be a great political figure—the capacity to command loyalty among his followers, the ability to organize brilliantly, to relate to all the people in his command, and even a social conscience of sorts, although his ideas of social justice are not precisely what I would be looking for in an elected official. I didn't voice that last item, but Mitsuru-san must have liked the rest of it because he beamed broadly and directly at me, then rose abruptly from the table and left to make a phone call. Mr. Chang and I made little okay signs with our thumbs and forefingers, and a few moments later Mitsuru-san was back smiling graciously. "I have spoken with my father," he said, "and he says he will be pleased to receive you in his home in Kobe next Sunday at this time."

Mission accomplished, we all relaxed into small talk, and I violated all the rules about getting personal. Taking advantage of my advanced age, I asked him about his schooling (it had been a drag), about girls (plentiful at the time, but he has since plucked one beauty from the crowd and married her), whether he had ever visited the United States (he had, but when I met his father, would I please not bring it up as he had cut out of school for a few weeks to make the trip and it was still a very sore point), and so on. We even got into politics, I think because Watergate was Topic A everywhere in the world at the time.

This was a rather dodgy area for I was well briefed on the ultraconservative political views of the *yakuza*, and I have always had a bad habit of getting feisty in political arguments, but I managed to keep my cool while Mitsuru-san explained his father's views to me, which sounded as though his father's politics were slightly to the right of Marie Antoinette's. Japan is basically conservative, but apparently Taoka senior feels that creeping socialism is ruining the country, and is aided and abetted by the press and by the ruling clique in government which, according to him, are both very soft on communists. "Ummm," I kept commenting wisely. The *yakuza*, Mitsuru-san said, were actually a bulwark against the excesses of the left, stalwart defenders of traditional values in Japan. I pricked up my ears at that and my mind raced around picturing one hundred and fifty thousand well-armed, well-disciplined, highly motivated men. Clearly they could be quite an effective bulwark if they had a mind to become one. A poker face is not one of my better-known accomplishments, and Mitsuru-san, noting my expression, issued a gentle backhand warning about how to behave with his father. Half smiling, he said, "One thing I really do envy

Americans. They can say what they think to one another and still remain friends."

"And that is not possible in Japan?" I asked.

He shook his head. "No, not possible." Mr. Chang smiled. It was what he had been telling me right along.

To change the subject, I think, Mr. Chang reminded me that I had brought a copy of my book, *The Scarlett Letters*, to show to Mitsuru-san. It had been Mr. Chang's suggestion that I bring it, I rather imagine for the purpose of demonstrating that I was a solid working citizen, and not simply an adventuress who travels across continents and oceans for a rendezvous with gangsters. I opened the book to the pictures, which made it possible for Mitsuru-san and me to communicate without benefit of interpreter.

"Ah," he would say, pointing to a member of the cast, "Takarada-san!"

"*Hai!*" I would reply, "Takarada-san!"

Never mind. It may not have been a brilliant exchange, but it demonstrated that we had friends in common, which changed my status from total unknown quantity to someone who could be checked if need be. I pointed with pride to my husband and Mitsuru-san clucked admiringly and said that he knew him by reputation as a distinguished composer, which put a smug smile on my face. His next remark instantly wiped it off. He told me that he personally had an unfortunate tendency to sleep through most shows and so did not attend them, in deference to many of his clients who were performers and who begged him to stay away.

All in all I was lulled into complacency by the comparative smooth sailing of our meeting until a small cloud made its appearance on the horizon just as we were taking leave of each other. There was just one thing, Mitsuru-san told Mr. Chang, a matter of the business arrangements. When my book was published, he would like my assurance that he would have the right to select a translator, and also he would like to be given the rights to its distribution. It did not sound so much like a request as like an offer I couldn't refuse, and I'm afraid a slight edge crept into my tone when I pointed out that it was not within my province to assign such rights. I also told Mr. Chang to tell him that I thought it would decrease the value of anything I might have to say if it were known that he was involved, for would it not appear that I had been bribed to write a book showing his father in a favorable light? He waved that aside as though I were speaking woman nonsense.

"When you really understand about the *yakuza*," he said, "you will write favorably about them if you are an honest person. And when you meet my father you will be able to judge for yourself that he is a great man. In any case, I would ask you to approve the translator I would select."

Big deal. As though I would be capable of judging the merits of one translator against another. Mr. Chang signaled that I should not make an issue of this, so I took my cue and said merely that I was sure we could reach an agreement and I wished he were *my* agent. He bowed politely, waved a cheery goodbye and called, "*Dewa matta* (see you later)" as he took off. I bowed back and called "See ya" to his retreating back. Our little meeting had taken up the better part of the afternoon, what with all the translating and leisurely lunching and pussyfooting, and the fact that I was auditioning for and being judged by a young man whom I considered to be a mere stripling had taken quite a toll on my nerves. I was exhausted, and somewhat worried by the fact that I should be so tired at the very beginning of my *yakuza* hunt.

I spent the intervening week before my meeting with Taoka senior cramming on *yakuza*. Mitsuru-san had said that they have a long and honorable tradition. Well, it's long all right. When I had learned of a Japanese mafia I had jumped to the immediate conclusion that it had been imported from America, like baseball. Looking at the structure, it certainly *seemed* to be a faithful reproduction, operating in a network of crime "families," each such family dominated by a strong father image, a rigidly maintained hierarchy, larded with rituals and firmly maintained rules of conduct. Conclusion-jumping in Japan is an unrewarding sport, I learned, and you are apt to fall flat on your face most of the time.

I found out my error in conversation with Bernard Krisher, who smiled when I stated my view. "But you see," he said, "that's the structure of the entire Japanese society. You're mistaken if you think the *yakuza* got their operational techniques from watching *Little Caesar* or *Scarface*. They follow the pattern of their own families, or business or any institution you want to name in Japan. They're not the descendants of Sicilian peasants, remember. They're Japanese. And they've been around a lot longer than the mafia."

As a matter of record, the *yakuza* have been on the scene in Japan for more than three hundred years, which not only predates our mafia—it predates our history as a nation. The only thing about them which is fairly recent is their name—*yakuza*—and of course, they've had to change some of their methods of operating because, like the rest of the country, they've had to fit themselves into the industrial age. Just the same, they are actually more committed to old customs and traditions than the legitimate society, and some of their resistance to change has its frightening aspects. The mainstream of Japanese life is not interested in a return to feudalism, but with the *yakuza* it's quite another matter.

"You can hardly blame them for that," said my next appointment, Arthur Miyazawa, who teaches at a leading university, "for in a sense that was their finest hour. Don't forget that they think of themselves as the spiritual descendants of the samurai." But the samurai, I argued, were supposed to have been a noble class. "Yes, you could say that," said Mr. Miyazawa, "but there are some cynics who see many of them as having been the hired guns of their time. They were, after all, warriors who were in the pay of landlords, hired to protect their property. The feudal lords were constantly at war with each other, which meant that somebody had to win and somebody had to lose. The losers put a lot of samurai defenders out of work, so what were they going to do with themselves? They weren't equipped for much more than fighting, most of them, and there were those who organized themselves into mobs, you might say, and wandered around preying on the countryside, looting and terrorizing the merchants and farmers. Don't be too hard on them, though. They were as much victims of the times as the people they victimized."

When the Tokugawa period began in Japan at the outset of the seventeenth century, a consolidation of power put an end to the civil strife. Among the samurai, however, particularly those who were out of work, there was a lot of strong feeling about the "loss of warrior values," and they became the reactionary right-wingers of their time, unable to adjust to the new, comparatively peaceful era. They secretly trained themselves with strict discipline, adopted a distinctive style of dress and bound themselves to each other with oaths of loyalty. To be absolutely fair, there *was* a considerable amount of government repression, not just against the former nobles who had become bandits but against the common people, and legends which are now celebrated in song, story, classic drama and the cinema concern themselves less with their antisocial behavior than with the Robin Hood activities of the early outlaws. When the samurai disappeared at the end of the seventeenth century, they passed the legends and their style down to newer groups who replaced them and enshrined them as heroes. Well, we do the same thing, don't we? Look at that lovable old curmudgeon, *The Godfather*, and those high-spirited kids, *Bonnie and Clyde*. Just you wait, Lucky Luciano wherever you are, you'll get your victim-of-society status just like Jesse James and Billy the Kid.

I spent the entire week rounding up every bit of information dealing with *yakuza*, past and present, which I could lay hands on. I spoke with anyone who had a scrap of information to add to the heap I had accumulated—criminologists, journalists, sociologists, theoreticians—and with a few lower-echelon *yakuza* who weren't all that hard to meet if you happened to have a wide acquaintance among theater people. The net result of all that nonstop talking and listening was that in addition to wearing me out, "word" got around.

I had two cryptic phone calls from friends, one of whom owns a restaurant and consequently has had his share of problems with *yakuza,* but who has a few friends among them too, and the other from an actor who gets around in low circles because he loves to gamble. The gist of both conversations was "What in hell are you up to? I've been asked questions about you by some very peculiar people who found out I know you." I said it was a small world, and they told me it was smaller than I thought and that I should keep my nose clean and not do anything foolish. Obviously somebody was checking on me too, a fact which I found more amusing than frightening.

Mitsuru-san was waiting for us in the lobby of the Oriental Hotel in Kobe at the appointed time. He seemed a bit preoccupied as we made our way to the coffee shop, and I had barely started munching on a greasy ham-and-egg sandwich when he started cross-examining me again.

"Did you come to Japan with your mind already made up about *yakuza?*" he asked. By now I was a little weary of the Lo! The Noble *Yakuza* theme, the sandwich wasn't very good, I'd had that long hot trip, and I regret to say that my tact was wearing a little thin.

I sighed and said, "If I'd had any fixed ideas I wouldn't be sitting here. I'd have saved my money and stayed in my nice comfortable apartment on Fifth Avenue in New York City and invented the whole thing. It was my earnest desire to be fair and to be accurate that brought me here." Very well then, he conceded, in that case there was a little further business to discuss.

He had made a note of my publisher's name the previous week, and the publishing company will be pleased to learn that he had a good report on it as a perfectly reputable organization. Since this was true, he was sure that my publisher would agree that in return for "their" cooperation, "they" should have a reasonable percentage of royalties. Say eight to ten percent off the top on every book sold, plus fifty percent of the movie rights. Mr. Chang explained it all, deadpan, as though it were a perfectly ordinary and reasonable condition, adding for my benefit that I mustn't look upset. The truth is that I was rather flattered. Apparently they were thinking in terms of a gold mine and of me as a substantial contributor to the fortunes of the Yamaguchi-gumi. I said that I had no authority to make any deals, since that is the province of the publisher. However, I added, I would be glad to offer them a share of my own royalty, whatever they thought would be fair.

Mitsuru-san brushed that aside grandly. No, I was entitled as a hard-working writer to everything that was coming to me. In fact, were it up to him alone, he said, he would gladly tell me everything I wanted to know just as a favor and proof of friendship. However, it was not up to him alone, and his father's rights and the rights of the organization had to be protected. Would I therefore get in touch with my publisher and get back to "them" with the decision? And, I asked him, what if my publisher did not agree?

"In that case," he said, "my father will tell you nothing, nor will anyone else in any of the organizations affiliated with the Yamaguchi-gumi."

I turned to Mr. Chang. "I don't like to sound dramatic," I said, "but it sounds to me as though he's saying that if I don't get up the protection money they'll break the windows in my store and put me out of business."

He smiled. "Don't be so serious," he said. "We have lots of time to discuss business arrangements later. Just tell him you'll put in a call to New York."

"Okay," I said, "but in that case what are we doing in Kobe? Is he going to call off our date with his old man?"

He spoke to Mitsuru-san, who wrestled with the problem for a moment and then got up from the table. I thought for a shattered moment it was to abandon us, but he said, "Let's go. You may visit my father this afternoon, but keep in mind that this is a social occasion. Under no circumstances are you to use a tape recorder, and you will take no pictures or make any notes." He repeated it to make sure we both understood, and off we went.

As the Taoka car sped to the house, I reviewed the improbable circumstances which had begun to resemble a comic opera—a middle-aged housewife from New York being intimidated by a gangster's son and driving to an assignation with a man whose record was studded with mayhem and murder. May I hastily add that I felt no fear for my personal safety. I've never met a gangster who didn't behave like a choir boy in the presence of us "good" women. And to be fair to Mitsuru-san, once he had taken care of his business conditions, he couldn't have been more amiable. He told me about the movie he was producing—his first—and his trials and tribulations with labor costs and other woes. He even asked me about my husband's availability to do a score for a picture at some future time, and I'm sure his intention was to put me at my ease. Mr. Chang too was murmuring comforting asides to me, such as "Don't worry, you'll be able to think of a few questions you can sneak into the chitchat," but just the same I felt angry and frustrated.

The ignition was barely switched off when Mitsuru-san leaped out of the car and disappeared into the house, leaving me and Mr. Chang to the tender mercies of the crew-cut quartet of *yakuza* guards. They were enormously polite and a little awkward, trying not to show their surprise at the odd couple we must have seemed to them. As they escorted us in, Mr. Chang whispered to me, "You'll be surprised at how much you can learn about Taoka-san. Don't forget, everyone enjoys talking about himself."

I don't know about everybody, but I suppose that's generally true. Besides, Taoka-san is a star, and what star can resist a genuine fan—one who has traveled halfway around the world to meet him? At least I hoped that was how it would work out.

We were ushered into the living room, and the quartet bowed like a team of vaudeville acrobats, exited and closed the door behind them. I watched their retreating backs, and only regretted that they were wearing those T-shirts, because I assumed that under them they bore the trademark of the *yakuza*, elaborate body tattoos.

"I wonder if they are," I said to Mr. Chang.

"Are what?" he asked.

"Tattooed," I replied.

He shrugged. "Most probably," he said.

"And what about our host?" I wanted to know.

"Again, probably—but if I were you, that's not one of the questions I'd try to sneak in."

The tradition of tattooed gangsters is one which fascinates me. *Yakuza* tattoos are not to be spoken of in the same breath with the kind which American seamen are sometimes given to—the two-hearts-entwined with I Love Rosie variety. The *yakuza* get themselves tattooed starting at the collar in an all-over pattern which sometimes covers their bodies clear down to the ankles. The patterns are influenced by the patterns in samurai dress, especially the *haori* (jacket) and *kamishimo* (old ceremonial dress), and most particularly when dragons and other dramatic or heroic symbols were used.

In the feudal period the tattoo appeared as a mark of punishment, and criminals were generally tattooed with one black ring around the arm for each offense. As suppression by the ruling class touched a great many people who were not criminals, tattooing grew to be a symbol of resistance to despotism, especially as tattooing was forbidden by law. Because it was such a test of strength to endure the pain of tattooing, it began to take on other aspects—manliness, courage, health, vitality and so on—and the *yakuza* in adhering to this custom feel themselves to be the possessors of such attributes.

The tattooing is generally done on a dark background to make the patterns stand out more vividly, which means predyeing the skin. The pattern is then put on, sometimes to the elbow and waist, downward to the knee, and even to the ankle, making what appears to be a skin-tight, lacy garment. Some women do it too, the women who belong to *yakuza* circles and a few kooks, although I doubt there are "his" and "hers" patterns. The lady *yakuza* patterns run more frequently to flowers and leaves and quiet figures of Buddha, with maybe a serpent or so entwined throughout. As of now, tattooing is associated chiefly with *yakuza*, but there are a few non-*yakuza* here and there who have done it for kicks and to show off how tough and hardy they are.

We were permitted to browse in Taoka's receiving room for a quarter of an hour by ourselves, probably to give me a chance to take in my luxurious surroundings. Actually it wasn't all *that* luxurious, but it was certainly comfortable-looking, and I noted with relief that there was a Western-type black leather sofa and chairs. Had I been obliged to sit on the floor on my haunches in Japanese fashion, it would have taken the combined strength of all those gangster escorts to get me up again that day.

The room was not what a cultivated Japanese would call *shibui*, which I interpret as meaning exquisite and usually understated taste, but neither was it ticky-tacky in a *nouveau riche* way. It was the house of a prosperous suburban businessman who had scorned the services of a decorator, preferring to rely on his own taste and to surround himself with memorabilia. There were some beautiful teakwood tables and cabinets, on one of which was a collection of miniature carved elephants; there was the mandatory big color TV set; some oils and sculptures; and dozens of trophies—offerings, I was told by Mr. Chang, from devoted followers to show their appreciation for all Taoka-san had done for them. A silver golfing trophy which stood waist-high was hung with strips of calligraphy expressing sentiments of affection, a miniature *yagura* (tower) from sumo wrestlers, indicating their close relationship with Taoka and the Yamaguchi-gumi, and so on. It was an impressive array of testimonials to a leading pillar of the community who had earned the love and respect of his fellow citizens.

When we had been given sufficient time to nose around, the crew-cuts reappeared to stand at attention as the Taoka family—mother, father and son—entered. I stood riveted while Mr. Chang stepped forward, bowed and thanked them for allowing us to come. It takes a long time to say almost anything in Japanese with all the *politesse* which is involved, and it gave me the opportunity to collect myself and to memorize the details of Taoka's appearance, since I would not be allowed to photograph him.

There was certainly nothing menacing in the appearance of this pale man who looked as though he were recuperating from a long illness—which indeed he was. His oxford gray silk suit hung rather loosely on him, and above the white turtleneck sweater his neat, small head was perched forward in an attentive listening attitude as Mr. Chang spoke. His eyes, narrow and intelligent, never for a moment strayed in my direction, and his mouth seemed always on the verge of smiling, upturned by nature at the corners. When he finally did smile, when Mr. Chang had finished speaking, it was a curious lopsided smile, as though he had been caught with his fingers in the jam, and very disarming. I suppose my impression of him was based on what I already knew about him, but he really did exude a feeling of enormous and contained power, even with the pallor of his recent illness. *Take it easy*, I told myself, *don't get swept away. This isn't exactly Dr. Schweitzer you're meeting. It's more like Dr. No.* I let my eyes fall to his well-manicured hands, and just to break the spell I made myself wonder whether they could still wield a long sword and stick it through someone's gut.

With the barest of nods, he signaled the guard, who disappeared silently, and then turned his attention to me. Mitsuru-san cleared his throat and did the honors. Using up his entire command of the English language he said, "Mrs. Rome, I would like to present to you my mother and my father."

Not to be outdone, I bowed and said, *"Hajimema-shita,"* which I had learned was proper on the occasion of meeting someone for the first time, and we all laughed self-consciously at one another's erudition. Mrs. Taoka, plump, attractive and motherly, set a tray-ful of glasses filled with a dark liquid refreshment on the teakwood table in front of the sofa. I could have been visiting friends in Scarsdale up to this point, except for the language. However, unlike Scarsdale, I had a host-ess who knew her place, believe you me, and who got out as soon as she had deposited her tray. She was to return from time to time, bearing cakes, tea, melon—always silently, always with the same self-effacing bow. I think the only time I heard her voice was on one of her exits, when Mitsuru-san gave her an affectionate pat on the fanny and she looked over her shoulder at him fondly, murmuring something which I took to be the Japanese equivalent of "naughty boy!" There is some-thing about Japanese women which makes Western women feel brash and loud-mouthed, even when they're cowed and weary as I was at that moment.

Taoka's voice, low and gravelly, reached me, welcom-ing me to his house and inviting me to sit down just in time to keep me from caving in at the knees. Mr. Chang and I took our places on the sofa, and Taoka *père* and *fils* faced us in the chairs on the other side of the coffee table. The elder Taoka handed me my glass of the dark mysterious liquid (Pepsi-Cola, as it happened) and I noted with some surprise that his hand was shaking.

"Does he have Parkinson's disease?" I asked Mr. Chang out of the side of my mouth, and he replied, "No, I don't believe so. I told you about his heart condition."

"So why is his hand shaking?" I asked.

"Oh that," he replied, "well, as you are the first Westerner—and a woman at that—to be in this house, he's probably a little nervous at meeting you."

I was astonished, of course, and rather pleased. *He* was nervous? The thought comforted me, and I looked forward to putting this notorious gangster at his ease. Raising my glass in his direction I said, *"Kampai* (cheers)!" and downed my Pepsi while I tried to think of something to say to start the ball rolling. Mitsuru-san was sitting there like a watchdog, at least I felt he was, and I figured I'd better avoid cue words such as prostitution, gambling, extortion, blackmail or any of the other public services for which the Yamaguchi-gumi is famous. I covered the weather, the trip down, the scenery, and then, my eyes lighting on the elephant collection, I asked the elder Taoka whether there was any particular significance in his having chosen them to collect.

"Yes," he said, "they are a symbol of longevity."

It figured. People in risky professions are more apt than most to go around propitiating any gods in charge of prolonging life. As he was explaining this to me, he lit a cigarette and I found myself blurting out, "Taoka-san, all the elephants in the world aren't going to help you if you insist on smoking when you have a heart condition! Do you know what you're doing to your circulation?" I took a deep drag of the cigarette I was smoking and won a broad lopsided smile. "I know," I said, "but I intend to quit as soon as I get back to New York."

Taoka's hand began to shake less and he sounded quite relaxed as he said, "You sound just like my wife and all those doctors. At my age a man has to have *some* pleasures."

I drew myself up. "I have read much about you," I said, "so I happen to know that we are just about the same age, and I am still capable of enjoying many pleasures!"

He looked at me with, I'm pleased to say, some interest. "What do you suggest I do?" he asked. "I am forbidden any strenuous exercise, and I seldom leave this house . . ." I launched into a lecture on the beneficial results of yoga (which I'm too lazy to do with any regularity myself), explaining that he could do this right in his house, and got so carried away that I illustrated a few simple breathing exercises. With any encouragement I'd have stood on my head.

Mitsuru-san was lulled by these harmless goings-on, and indicating him with a gesture I said to his father, "Your son says you are a very great man."

He smiled and replied, "What choice does he have? I am his father."

"You'd be surprised," I said. "In America we have something called a generation gap. It's quite fashionable for young people to explain to their parents what

a mess they've made of the world." I expounded a bit
on the youth cult and told him about some of the words
which had crept into the vocabulary during the '60s
such as drop-out, alienation, doing-one's-thing and
other depressing phrases.

His eyes narrowed into slits. "Here too there has
been some of that," he said, "among our young people.
Old traditions mean less and less to them, and they are
encouraged to behave without respect or dignity by the
lax attitudes of the teachers, and some people in the
government and . . . (he looked pointedly at Mr. Chang,
who smiled enigmatically) . . . the newspapers and
magazines which pay less and less attention to Japanese
values. They say we must become more 'modern' and
liberalize our customs."

I was delighted to see him warm to this subject, for
I hoped it would lead him into an area where he would
talk about the *yakuza* involvement in politics. "Do you
know," he said, leaning forward earnestly in his chair,
"what the result of all this so-called freedom and liber-
alism has been?" I shook my head. "Wild inflation and
growing disorder. And do you know who profits from
such situations?"

I thought it over, then replied "Communists?" like a
good student.

"Exactly," he said. "They are the ones who know how
to capitalize on the miseries of people. What this country needs is a controlled economy and a cleaning out,
to purify and rid the nation of the disease of socialism."

The recurrent theme with all who talked to me about
yakuza was their extremist right-wing political view. It
seemed logical to me that they would have such a thing,
for they have a hefty stake in maintaining the status

quo. They would have a very great deal to lose if, to mention just one example, a truly modern labor-management operation were to take root. In some economically marginal industries, workers can be forced to work for bare subsistence levels as loyal *kobun* to their labor-racketeering *oyabun*. The heads of such industries find it to their distinct advantage to use the *yakuza* to enforce their labor policy, and to label any dissident workers as "red," and it follows that they support those elements in politics with whom they see eye-to-eye economically, as do the *yakuza*. However, while dragging out the specter of communism may be a cynical ploy, Taoka did impress me as being absolutely sincere in regarding it as the danger which threatens the country, and the *yakuza*, as Mitsuru-san had said, as the bulwark against it. Not wishing to be drummed out of the house by Mitsuru-san, I didn't argue the point.

Instead, I made a tentative stab in the direction of religion, remarking that his views, particularly those about "purity" and "old traditions and values," seemed to be in line with those of Soka Gakkai, the religious movement which claims ten million followers. Until that year Soka Gakkai had had as its political arm the third-largest political party in Japan, the Komeito (Clean Government Party), and had only recently cut its direct tie. Taoka nodded and said that he had indeed, prior to his last heart attack, made arrangements to meet with Daisaku Ikeda, who is the spiritual leader of the Soka Gakkai movement, but had called it off when he became ill.

"In the meanwhile," he said, "I lost interest in them because they severed their relationship with the Komeito and both branches became ineffective." (They must have come to the same conclusion since that time, because I understand that they have reaffiliated.)

"Yes," I said, "but why would you have wanted to meet with him in the first place?"

He smiled. "They seem to have a very great talent for recruiting membership," he said, "and I thought perhaps I could learn something from them. My organization is very small compared to theirs. And of course, they do have a very interesting point of view."

I do not wish to hint at any sinister relationship between gangsters and Soka Gakkai (which translates as Value Creating Society). What they have in common is a conservative political outlook, but they carry out their purposes in quite different ways. The Soka Gakkai, in fact, calls itself "revolutionary," but the revolution they advocate is one of the soul, and the reactions I had heard to this dynamic organization ranged all the way from tolerance and amused condescension from sophisticates, to deep hostility from the political left, which sees all that chanting and prayer as a camouflage for teaching compliance—a colossal con game conceived for the purpose of mesmerizing people into inaction toward improving their lot.

Taoka's remark, by the way, sent me scurrying up to the foot of Mount Fuji several weeks later for a tour of Sho-Honda, which is the headquarters of the movement. From what I saw, I don't blame Taoka for being impressed. It is a vast and lavish complex, with quarters for housing thousands of pilgrims, a shrine which accommodates five thousand (each seat having an individual loudspeaker and air conditioner built in), an art museum filled with Oriental treasures, and several plush administration buildings. I came with a VIP and got some fallout VIP treatment myself, which was a bit of a mixed blessing. The complex covers thousands of acres, and while I was honored to be given such special treatment, with my own guide who was in their public relations department, plus a young barefoot priest, their zeal and proselytizing fervor were such that we had covered a considerable number of those acres before they noticed that I was beginning to buckle.

The Soka Gakkai would seem not to have any need of the Yamaguchi-gumi or any other gangster organization to enforce their point of view. They're doing very well on their own, but it struck me as curious that Mr. Ikeda would agree to a meeting with a known criminal of the stature of Taoka. Perhaps as a spiritual leader he had felt it his duty to try to steer him into the paths of righteousness, who knows? Nevertheless the gangsters of Japan stand ready to offer their services to any right-minded people in the event of confrontation, and there are considerable numbers of such people who stand ready to use them. Nonsense? Yes indeed. What legitimate organization would make a deal with gangsters? That's almost as ridiculous as the notion that a racket-busting governor like Dewey of New York would commute the sentence of a notorious criminal, for instance Lucky Luciano, with the explanation that he had performed invaluable wartime service by organizing the underworld dock mobs to combat sabotage. Far-out. But it happened.

At this stage of his life Taoka-san is convinced that everything he has ever done has been motivated by duty and obligation. "I have lived my entire life on one principle," he said, "that of *giri.*" Every time I heard that word it took on another nuance. From simple "duty" and "obligation," it gathered a mystic force which once it was undertaken seemed to go on forever. The ties of *giri* seem stronger than the ties of marriage or parents and children, and I felt that Taoka's *giri* extended to each of his ten thousand members. I commented that it sounded like a full-time job.

"In English," I said, "we have a similar expression, 'one hand washes the other.' " I left out the rather cynical connotation and Mr. Chang translated it at some length as Mitsuru-san listened closely.

All three of the men went through the pantomime of washing their hands, with a great many "ahs!" from Taoka-san as he got the drift that one hand would not get clean without assistance and encouragement from the other. At the end he said, "That is a very vivid expression. I like it. Would you mind if I were to use it?"

"Please be my guest," I said. (In future, if you run across groups of *yakuza* hand-wringing at one another, you'll know where it came from. I like to think of having made a contribution to the colorful argot of the *yakuza* world.)

The retired-country-gentleman aura which Taoka-san gave off didn't square with what I knew about him, but it was obviously true that he seldom left his house. I asked him how he was able to keep up his contacts, and he replied, "Many people come here to consult me."

"Hmmm," I commented, "like Bernard Baruch," and Mr. Chang had to go through that one, about the park bench where the elder statesman sat dispensing advice to the government officials who sought him out. Taoka-san rather liked the analogy, and I asked him what they consulted him about. Mitsuru-san looked alert, but he needn't have worried. His old man could give him lessons in diplomatic double talk.

"I am not without knowledge about securing financing in difficult situations. With the present state of inflation, motion picture companies, to mention one example, sometimes find that their picture budget has not allowed for rising costs. I happen to have many friends among film people, and it is natural for them to think of me when they have such problems, for I have had considerable experience in securing additional financing and in cutting corners and so forth." He made it all sound very philanthropic, so naturally I wondered how he kept this estate going by dispensing free advice, and I felt a little regretful that his generous attitude did not extend to struggling writers. I didn't mention it.

Taoka-san rose, which I thought at first was a royal dismissal, but not at all. He wanted to show me some of his treasures. "You haven't seen my newest gift," he said to Mr. Chang, and we followed him up a few stairs into another room, and since we had to take off the slippers we were wearing, I assumed it was a ceremonial room of some kind. He pointed proudly to a suit of samurai armor in a glass case against the wall. It was in mint condition and probably worth a fortune, and we all oohed and aahed with admiration. With a touch of wonder he said, "What surprises me most is that they were such *small* men."

With a spot of craven boot-licking I replied, "Yes, but from what I have read they were very large in spirit and courage."

"That is true," said their spiritual descendant as he

pointed out some other samurai artifacts on a wall—a long pole and a sword.

"Do you know how to use them?" I asked as if I didn't know. He shrugged modestly.

In all we spent about three hours chatting and drinking tea and eating melon (and at twelve bucks a melon, which was the going price, I knew I was getting the A Treatment) and the word *yakuza* never came into the conversation. When Mr. Chang and I rose to start the long homeward trek, the *yakuza* guards appeared as if on cue, ready to escort us to the car.

"I hope I can see you again," I said as I bowed my thanks, and he replied, "I sincerely hope it can be arranged."

I wouldn't have been a bit surprised if he meant it. I was as much an oddity in his life as he was in mine, when you stop to think about it, and I said, "I'll discuss it with your son the agent."

It could certainly have been an afternoon with any public-spirited, patriotically motivated citizen of high moral principle, and nothing he said made me change my opinion that with a few alterations in the circumstances of his early life, Kazuo Taoka had the talent to become a distinguished prime minister. On the plane trip home, I said to Mr. Chang, "Heart attack or no, he's still *numero uno,* isn't he?"

Mr. Chang nodded. "And he will be until they carry him out," he said, "if that's the way he wants it." This feeling was reinforced through scores of other people —*yakuza, yakuza*-related and non-*yakuza*—who, despite all those warnings from Mitsuru-san, were absolutely delighted to tell me everything-I-wanted-to-know-but-was-afraid-to-ask about the Japanese mafia, both before and after I had met Taoka-san.

CHAPTER 3

IN THOSE sometimes lurid reminiscences which he himself did for the *Asahi Geino*, Kazuo Taoka refers to himself as "Yamaguchi-gumi the Third," meaning that he is the third *oyabun* to head the organization, and the first one who is not in the direct blood line. The original *oyabun* was named, logically enough, Yamaguchi, and *gumi* means group or association. Yamaguchi had been a fisherman in Kobe in the early 1920s and he saw a way of getting ahead by organizing fifty-odd vagrants and hooligans along the waterfront and becoming a labor boss. The men he organized were untouchables in the legitimate labor market, and their needs were slight—a bowl of rice, a place to flop, and a few yen left over for cheap whisky. Yamaguchi furnished them with the *gonzo-heya* (lodging room) and the fifty mats on which they slept, in return for which he took a percentage of their earnings. It wasn't illegal, and there were plenty of racketeers along the waterfront doing the same thing, supplying cheap labor to employers who were not too fussy about references.

"That kind of recruiting goes on today too," said Nakamura-san, my young socialist informant who had been sent to me by an editor of one of the newspapers. ("Perhaps if you give him lunch at the Imperial Hotel," he had suggested tactfully. "His own finances don't allow for such splendor." I did, with pleasure. We had blintzes, a specialty of the room in which we lunched!) "If I were to take you over to the construction site where some big building project is going on, or down to the docks," he continued, "you'd see perhaps a few thousand men lining the streets to the Labor Exchange at five o'clock in the morning, hoping to get a day's work."

"I thought," I said, "that there was actually a labor shortage now."

"In some areas, yes," he said, "but these are not skilled workers, and I'm afraid they're not exactly desirable people either. The Labor Exchange can take care of some of the more reliable people, but most of the recruiting is being done on the street by *yakuza*. Anyway the workers would rather deal with them."

"Why?" I asked.

"You have to understand," he said, "mostly they come from the same background." (Just what I had heard about the entertainment world, I thought.) I asked him if he *would* take me to such a construction site and he almost gagged. "I would not like to be responsible for bringing a *gaijin* among so many rough characters." I didn't press him, and he grew earnest with socialist fervor. "What they do not understand, the workers and *yakuza* who work directly for the companies themselves, is that they are both simply tools of their exploiters."

The original Yamaguchi showed great talent in labor recruitment. His rivals in the field were an assortment of two-bit *oyabuns* of other gangs in control of various rackets, and they were busily knocking each other off in a struggle for whatever action existed. The shrewdest of these was a man named Oshima, who manipulated things to keep the feuds going and was in a fair way toward becoming the big boss of the territory by the time Yamaguchi entered the picture. Oshima figured him correctly to be too formidable to deal with in the usual way, so instead he invited him to join forces, which he did. Who got the upper hand eventually can only be judged by the fact that it is called the Yamaguchi-gumi and not the Oshima-gumi.

All this happened in 1926, at which time Kazuo Taoka was only fourteen years old and had never heard of the Yamaguchi-gumi, nor had he any concept of the role he would play in building this mangy little group of cussing, drunken hoodlums into a disciplined force of ten thousand men.

He was born on March 28, 1912, in Tokushima prefecture, in a village called Sanshomura, which is on the island of Shikoku, just across the strait from the bustling city of Kobe. Sanshomura didn't bustle. It lay quietly and peacefully along the banks of the Yoshino River and extended back into the woods and mountains, wildly beautiful. Taoka's memories are not of the lyric beauty of his environment which inspired poets and brush drawings of artists, but of unrelieved hardship and hunger and loneliness, desperate loneliness.

"There was just me and my mother," he recalls in *Yamaguchi-gumi Third Generation,* the story of his life, "for my father had been a poor peasant who died before I was born." There had been sisters and a brother, but the sisters were married and lived in another town, and his brother was apprenticed to a store in Kyoto. There were no family reunions in the old homestead, for even if such things had been a financial possibility, they would have been a most unusual departure from Japanese custom. In the structure of Japanese society, a daughter who is given into another household in marriage becomes a part of that household, and all her filial responsibility is transferred to her mother-in-law. Even a quarrel with her husband will not find her running home to mother for comfort, for that is no longer her "place," and her mother will be the first to point that out to her.

In the case of Taoka's mother, the fact that her daughters were married and taken care of was a great blessing, for she could barely feed herself and her only remaining dependent son. From daybreak until nightfall, she worked in the fields of a landowner, eking out a miserable existence for the two of them, filling their bowls with a mixture of rice and wheat and a few pickled vegetables. Extravagances such as milk or eggs were beyond speculation, and there was no time for even the

simple pleasures that were enjoyed by other villagers—
visits to the shrines on festival days, or to occasional
street fairs.

Too young for school and with no friends to play
with, Kazuo spent each day by himself, wandering
around in the hills, picking wild mulberries, waiting for
his mother to return from the fields bent with fatigue,
to feed him and put him to sleep. No playful little moth-
er-and-son games, no songs or stories to make him
laugh, for she had no strength or spirit for frivolity. And
though he had once been permitted to go with his
mother to the fields where she worked, he was no
longer allowed to do so, for the scolding of her employer still rang in his ears: "You're using that kid as an
excuse for loafing on the job!"

Taoka is not lugubrious about these beginnings, because if they sound like life imitating a soap opera,
that's the way things were in Japan not only for him, but
for the millions of other impoverished peasants. A police researcher to whom I went for some illumination
on Taoka's early life assured me that his was not an
unusual story for the times.

"We didn't call it feudalism any longer," he said,
"but in some segments of the society life went on as it
had under feudalism. I'm trying to think of something
comparable in your own country—sharecropping perhaps, in a way—although the landlord didn't furnish
Taoka's mother with a house or anything of that sort.
Technically she was an employee, but actually it was a
form of quasi-peonage. She had no recourse. It was do
as she was told or starve."

The booming affluence which was to startle the rest
of the world in the '60s was as yet undreamed of, and

although industrialization was beginning to spread and contact with the rest of the world was starting in the great cities of Tokyo, Kyoto and Kobe, none of the twentieth century had touched the sleepy little village of Sanshomura. Landlords and exploited peasants was still the way of life, but even in the rest of Japan the great wealth of the country was concentrated in the hands of elite groups: the aristocracy, the upper bureaucracy, big business interests, the military and the landed gentry. Taoka nurses no private sore spots that he was singled out for special abuse by fate. Far from being a bitter or rebellious child, he was shy and intro-spective. For all the murders and misdeeds which have since been laid at his door, that is the aura which he still seems to transmit.

In the winter before his fifth birthday, during the long, cold nights, his mother cut her sleeping time down to sew a new kimono and kimono skirt for little Kazuo which he would wear on the proud day when he entered primary school in the spring. It was the last present she would ever give him, for a few months later, as she stepped from her house to go to the fields, she collapsed from overwork. A doctor came once, shrugged and left, never to return. What medicine could he prescribe for poverty? Yet, though the circum-stances were desperate, his sisters and brother would not even answer the summons of neighbors who had sent telegrams. In his published account of these events, Taoka is not bitter even about this, for he un-derstands perfectly what their predicament was and bears them no grudge. The sisters were afraid of their mothers-in-law to whom they were virtual housemaids, as the mores of the society dictate, and his brother could not risk the loss of his job by being absent under any circumstances. They were not unusual circumstances, after all, for the poor of Japan.

The people who did come were the neighbors themselves, stealing time from their own arduous chores, bringing rice and soup from their meager cupboards. They tried to do what they could for the small, frightened boy, but there was nothing they could do for his mother. The machinery had given up. There came the day that she called Kazuo to her bedside to plead for forgiveness for not having been able to provide him with a better life, and to speak her last words: "Live bravely. I named you Kazuo because it means alone and brave." Alone he certainly was, but he was not quite up to bravery yet, and he ran from his house into the forest, pounded his fists and his head against a tree and wept bitterly.

The occasion of his mother's death and the attendant activity must surely have produced strange, conflicting emotions in the forlorn five-year-old boy. Suddenly, for the first time in his life, his house was filled with people. It was all curiously festive for so melancholy an event, and one can scarcely blame him for the guilty, secret excitement he felt. He surely could not help responding with pleasure to so many guests, all the relatives, all the feasting. He had never seen so much food all at one time, which the neighbors had brought. It was much more like a party—raised, excited voices, sake being drunk. The talk was endless, and chiefly about him or more specifically, about what was to be done with him. They patted him on the head and looked at him with sympathy, but it began to seep through to him that through all the talk ran the same hopeless, discouraging thread: "Of course I would take him if I could, but you understand that there is no room, there are so many of us, we cannot afford . . ." Before long he understood very well what they were saying. Nobody wanted him. They were not seeing him when they looked at him, they were seeing just another hungry belly, another responsibility to people who could barely shoulder their own. The one person who had cared what happened to him was gone, and later he was to suffer guilt at the thought that perhaps she could have had a longer and better life if she had not had to work herself to death on his account.

Much of the funeral sake had worked its way down the throat of his mother's brother, a jovial, irresponsible soul who lived and worked in Kobe. In a moment of wine-induced expansiveness, he scolded the other relatives for side-stepping what was clearly their duty and said, "I'm the only one here with any conscience! I'll take him home with me." Relieved, the other relatives gave him no time to sober up and reconsider this hasty decision, but kept refilling his cup with a vengeance as they made plans to pack up the scanty belongings of Kazuo and send the boy and his uncle on their way. Things had taken a turn for the better for little Kazuo. To his surprised delight he was to have a new family—this easy-going kindly uncle who would take him to the big city where there were so many people he would never again be lonely.

What he hadn't reckoned with was a not so kindly sour-faced aunt who wanted no part of him. No sooner had he stepped into the house than the fight was on. The now sober and sheepish uncle stood by while his wife berated him. What did he mean by bringing home this bedraggled wretch without so much as consulting her? Whom did he expect to look after him? Was it his thought that she would quit her job in the textile factory in order to stay home and wipe his nose? Her great lout of a husband had gone mad! It was an outrage and under no circumstances did she want that ragamuffin in her house! Her tirade seemed to go on endlessly, and Kazuo stood by helplessly, humiliated and guilty at being the cause of her venom and bitterly disappointed in his uncle for not standing up to her. He wanted to run away, but the strange city, so dazzling with its twinkling lights which had taken his breath away as he watched them from the rail of the boat on which he had arrived just a short time ago, was now a terrifying and unknown jungle to the quaking boy. There was nothing to do but to stand there, fighting back the tears which he knew it would be unmanly to display in front of anyone, until his aunt's rage had spent itself.

She did finally subside and ungraciously suffered him to stay, but Taoka, like a forest animal, now knew the areas he must avoid in order to remain safe from anger and punishment. There would be no carefree life of a child for him. He must tread softly, never get in anyone's way, never speak unless spoken to, never cause any accidents by breaking or spilling something, and he must bear the lash of his aunt's tongue even when he did not deserve it. Quiet by nature, he became doubly so. Now, however, it was a different kind of quiet. Now it was to cover the anger which had begun to build in him, for he dared not betray his true feelings under any circumstances. The process of tension, coiling up inside of him, had begun.

His aunt and uncle enrolled him in the local primary

school, where he became the butt of his classmates. This is not an uncommon status for "the new boy" in any school, but Kazuo, a shy and reticent country bumpkin, undersized and undernourished, and conditioned not to fight back, made no show of bravado against his tormentors as more secure "new boys" might do. He covered over the suppressed anger with mute patience, feeling that it was the only defense of the weak. He stayed silent, dreaming only of the day that he would grow up, earn his own living and somehow show them all! Now, however, his aunt nagged and complained daily about the cost of tuition, about the trouble it was to fix his lunch with which she sent him off to school each day, a lunch which was so unappetizing and scanty that he was ashamed to have the others see it and often threw it away and went hungry.

When he was ten years old he got a job as a newspaper delivery boy and proudly handed over the tiny amount he had earned to his uncle, to help pay for his tuition. It was his first experience with the sense of independence which the possession of money can bring, and hard on the heels of that experience came another, even more important ego-building event. When he was goaded beyond even his endurance by a senior classmate, the coil sprang and he reversed his pattern of standing meekly by. Without premeditation, he turned and attacked his enemy with hands and feet and to everyone's surprise, including his own, he won an astonishing victory over the bigger boy. His secret weapon had been motivation, a need for honor, and the ensuing prestige among his classmates. The brand-new feeling of self-esteem made him determine never to lose another fight. He never has.

So now he knew two things which he was never to forget all his life. He knew about money and he knew about muscle. The combination of the two could secure for him what his show of humility and meekness never had, and he began to feel his oats and do a bit of shoving around on his own. It turned out he was pretty good at that, and by the time he entered junior high school he had become quite a hero among his peers, and had developed a reputation of somebody with whom it was better not to fool around. With the littler kids he behaved differently, for he remembered his own experience as the class runt, and he felt it his duty to be protective of those who couldn't take care of themselves. He was, it would seem, beginning to exhibit the same quality of leadership which was to make him the most powerful *oyabun* of the underworld, by arbitrating fights among his juniors, making decisions for them, planning their recreations, listening to their problems. It was understood that he was their boss, and that they would do as he told them.

All of these circumstances could well have qualified him to grow up to be a successful businessman or political leader, but as luck would have it, among his classmates was one Hideo Yamaguchi. He was the second son of the original Yamaguchi *oyabun*, who had just died and whose place had been taken by his first son, Noboru Yamaguchi. Young Kazuo and Hideo were birds of a feather—like-minded, indifferent students—bright enough, but disinterested in the raptures of academic achievement. They became friends, and this fact shaped Kazuo's future.

Times were hard and there was widespread unemployment in Kobe in the year that Kazuo graduated from junior high school, but he managed to get a job in a shipyard as an apprentice lathe worker. His wages were minimal—not enough to feed or clothe himself, let alone pay his admission to an occasional movie—so he reluctantly continued to live under the roof of his sullen and unloving aunt and uncle, turning over to them whatever he earned.

By now Kazuo Taoka had completely abandoned the diffidence in his personality which had marked his earlier years and had replaced it with the violence which had been released in his first fight with a schoolmate. An apprentice lathe-worker status, in which he was expected to be subservient at all times to the petty despots who ordered him around, was bound to evoke that violence at some point, and it did. According to the hefty police dossier on Taoka, he didn't last very long on the job, but Taoka's own published version is that he was there for two years and that he left under dramatic circumstances: "One day I was helping out a fellow worker who was sick. My foreman shoved me and called me an idiot. I picked up a broom and hit him again and again. I didn't even know what I was doing until I heard everyone screaming, and then I ran out and never came back."

It was while he was roaming the streets looking for places to hide that his old school chum, Hideo Yamaguchi, ran across him, put an arm fraternally around his shoulders and led him to the *gonzo-heya* of the Yamaguchi-gumi. For all the filth and the stink of sweat and whisky, it was a warm and friendly atmosphere compared to the depressing aura of his uncle's house. The fifty-odd drunken, gambling hooligans who lived there accepted the seventeen-year-old boy as one of their own, teasing him with good humor and letting him watch their games and listen to their obscene sex talk. He never returned to his uncle's house—never even let them know where he was—nor did they send frantic bulletins to the police or organize search parties to find him. The year was 1929, and Kazuo Taoka had taken the first step toward becoming a *yakuza*.

The Yamaguchi-gumi was still pretty small potatoes in 1929. The likes of them could be found anywhere in Japan, some bigger and stronger, some weaker. As they had throughout their history, the *yakuza* lived in a world apart. One old-timer among them summarized their attitude in an interview with Bernard Krisher, in which he said, "In the old days, we used to remain in a corner of the public bathhouse to avoid splashing other people. When we walked down the street, we were told never to step on the shadow of other people. Whatever we did, we were never supposed to bother *katagi* (decent people)." They existed by running gambling games, practicing extortion on those on the fringes of the underworld, peddling drugs, smuggling, and their violence was directed against one another.

The *yakuza* in 1929 were a minor blight at best—certainly not in the same league with other "violence gangs" which were building up in Japan at that time, gangs which were not composed of gangsters in the accepted sense of the word. These were right-wing cliques of militarists who were plotting a policy of expansion abroad and a military takeover at home. Like the *yakuza*, they saw themselves as the inheritors of the

code of the samurai, and they gave their secret con-
spiratorial societies such names as the Heavenly Sword
Society, the Cherry Society, the Blood Brotherhood
and so on. They were given to violence and political
assassination, and it was these gangs rather than the
gangs of the underworld which were a thorn in the side
of the reasonable and law-abiding elements of the society.

The names have been dropped and the societies disbanded, but the ultranationalism which inspired them
is still very much in evidence in new societies which
have taken their place. As Taoka was drawn to the
yakuza, another boy who was exactly his age was attracted to the politics of the ultraright. His name was
Yoshio Kodama, and in their separate worlds, he and
Taoka were developing the forceful ideas which were to
make them both "godfathers"—Kodama the godfather
of the right, Taoka the godfather of the underworld.
Inevitably these two were to meet and to share a "cup
of brotherhood," but in 1929 Taoka hadn't a clue about
any of this, nor was he particularly interested in political
activities.

In 1929 he was still glorying in his new-found freedom from relatives and beginning to reap some of the
minor benefits of hanging around with petty grifters
and hoods: for example, free admission to cinemas and
theaters where the Yamaguchi-gumi had some clout,
for Noboru Yamaguchi had expanded his father's interests when he took over as *oyabun* to include a minor
incursion into show business. Just in a small way, of
course. He was supplying bouncers and various other
personnel to theater owners, but Taoka and his companions thought of it as their turf. Between hanging

around there and hanging around the *gonzo-heya*, his time was pretty well occupied, and he was learning from his companions. Not about politics, but about important matters such as gambling, sex, and the inexplicable ecstasy which could accompany violence.

He records that he was initiated into the last two items on the same night. The first, in a brothel located in the seamiest quarter of Kobe, filled him with self-loathing and disgust. For a boy who had listened to so much sex talk, he was curiously unprepared for what to expect. Certainly it had not been this malodorous, reeking house to which an older Yamaguchi-gumi member had taken him "to make a man of him." Because he did not dare to do otherwise, Taoka performed what was expected of him and then ran blindly into the rainy streets, not seeing or caring where he was heading, as long as it was far away from that hateful place. In his frantic, desperate wish to escape, he slid through a puddle of mud, splashing a passerby. A huge man to the skinny seventeen-year-old boy, he was actually about six feet tall as Taoka now remembers him, and built like a judo wrestler. He grabbed young Taoka by the scruff of the neck and throwing him to the ground, he shouted, "Who in hell do you think you're splashing, you punk!" A crowd began to gather, and Taoka was suffused with that familiar wave of rage and humiliation, just as he had been in school that day when he had been goaded into fighting. He banged his head against the barrel-like chest of his giant adversary and grappled with him desperately, the older man laughing at Kazuo's puny attempts to budge him.

Suddenly, to Kazuo's complete astonishment, the man fell to the ground, screaming with pain. His face was covered with blood, and Kazuo, bewildered by the turn of events, stared at him blankly. The crowd had begun to shrink back with horror, and Kazuo looked down at his own hands. They too were covered with blood. He was filled with the realization of what he had done; with these fingers at which he was staring, he had poked out the eyes of a man. Stunned, he watched his victim creep along the ground in agony, and as he turned to run, he trembled; not with revulsion for the monstrous nature of the act he had performed. He felt no horror. His emotion was excitement at his discovery that now he had a weapon against any foe—his own fingers. Taoka had charted his course. Brutality was now a way of life.

CHAPTER 4

BY THE TIME I met Kazuo Taoka, his days of gouging out eyes were far behind him. They seem not to weigh too heavily on his conscience, for though he will acknowledge that many of his acts were of an antisocial nature, he has an explanation for them which he seems to think was sufficient justification: "I was bursting with frustration."

I respond with horror to even pretended violence, so that I cannot sit through most of the films which pass for entertainment these days. When I am trapped into going to see one, there is no way anyone can pry my eyes open or unscrew my fingers from my ears while the mayhem is in progress. "Tell me when it's over," I hiss at my husband, and there have been films where I saw only the opening titles. I am told by savants that most people are capable of violence, given the proper provocation, and that part of being civilized is learning to suppress those feelings. It's lucky that there are more of us suppressors around than there are Taokas, or there wouldn't be enough jails to hold us all, for frustration is another emotion most of us in this world have experienced. Obviously, however, when Taoka and I talk about frustration, we're not talking about the same thing. The frustration which Taoka talks about is the kind that comes of being locked into a life situation from which there is no seeming escape—the life of hopelessness and poverty and discrimination that exists in the slums and ghettos of Japan (and of most other countries, including our own for that matter), which furnish the lush breeding places for criminals.

Yes, that's right, not every kid who comes out of a disadvantaged background grows up to be a hood. Not in the United States, not in Japan, not anywhere. As a matter of fact, it could be pointed out that another Japanese boy, a few years younger than Taoka, was also growing up in poverty at the same time. He was the son of a bankrupt and, it is rumored, drunken cattle farmer, and his name is Kakuei Tanaka, who broke the mold of establishment politics by becoming prime minister. As for Americans, we're fond of trotting out and pointing with pride to the hundreds of rags-to-riches Horatio Alger stories with which our past and current history is studded, and this brings up one of those cultural differences which I was constantly finding myself smack up against. The Japanese seem not to share our enthusiasm for men who pull themselves up by the bootstraps. They are members of a hierarchy (although not one arrived at by reasons of birth necessarily) and anybody who tries to change the organizational charts has a fight on his hands. The Japanese, with sensitive class-consciousness, demonstrate by word and gesture, even in their everyday contacts, their belief in the basic inequality of man. They bow lower and use honorific forms of address to those higher on the social ladder, and while I certainly do not deny that in our country too some of us seem to be a lot more equal than others, we do constantly enact civil rights legislation designed to erase our differences.

It's attitudes I'm talking about, not realities, for as an American urban dweller I know a little something about ghettos and poverty. However, it was Japanese ghettos I was chasing down, because of something Taoka had said to Mr. Chang: "So many of my people were born insecure." Mr. Chang had explained that he was referring to the *burakumin,* the people who live in the *buraku,* which are the ghettos of Japan. If you've never heard of them it's not surprising, because as with so many other unpleasant things which are bad for the national image, most Japanese don't like to talk about them. There are about three million *burakumin* living in approximately five thousand hamlets and enclaves scattered throughout Japan, and it isn't that their poverty is any worse than ours, it's that the social attitudes which surround them make their lives virtually unbearable.

To understand about the Japanese *yakuza,* you really do have to know something about the *burakumin* because that's where the bulk of them are drawn from. Sure, there are a few exceptions. Once in a very great while, someone of middle-class family—a drop-out from his background with psychological hang-ups of one kind and another, or a thrill-seeker—might be found in the ranks, but such exceptions are rare. The classic Japanese *yakuza* background is very different. Even Taoka does not completely qualify, for although he was reared in poverty, he is not the victim of either racial or social discrimination based on any condition of "previous servitude," as our own Constitution puts it.

It is not race which distinguishes the *burakumin* from their fellow countrymen. They are as Japanese as anyone else, and have in fact been called by sociologist George Devos "Japan's Invisible Race." It is "previous servitude" which is the joker in their case, and which has kept them in their ghettos since the sixteenth century, for they are the descendants of the *eta,* a class roughly comparable to the Indian untouchables.

"Tell me," I said to my patient university professor friend, Mr. Miyazawa, "about the *eta.*" In reply he held up four fingers. "What's that supposed to mean?" I asked.

"It is the symbol," he said, "for a four-legged animal. You see, at one time it was considered by Buddhists and Shintoists to be an abomination to earn a living by slaughtering animals. Or even by anything connected with animals, such as tanning hides or working with leather in any way. Just the same, these jobs had to be done, and so did lots of other lowly labors—executing criminals, working in cemeteries, and curiously enough, even making bricks and tiles. All these jobs were done by the *eta,* and even though we needed them so badly—couldn't, in fact, have gotten along without them—they were held in such low esteem that their masters would throw their pay in the dust and let them grovel for it so as to avoid the possibility of any body contact. An *eta* quite literally could be executed for allowing his shadow to fall in the path of his betters." Miyazawa-san stopped for a moment to draw me some Chinese picture symbols which are called *kanji* and which constitute much of the written language of Japan. He was writing *eta*, which broke up into *e*, meaning "contamination," and *ta*, meaning "much."

As he did so, he said, "Of course, you *do* realize that we officially outlawed the designation of the *eta* as a class a long time ago."

"So how come their descendants still live in the *buraku?*" I asked.

He never missed a beat. "How come your blacks and Puerto Ricans still live in ghettos?" he replied. "You ought to know it's not so easy to legislate prejudice out of existence."

I pointed out what I thought were great differences, the rapid changes which we are undergoing in employment practices, in housing and education, and he said, "So you're faster. Our democratic tradition is not so old and firmly established as yours, and there is, of course, the fact that we are all registered in the prefecture in which we were born with quite complete information as to our ancestry. It is difficult for anyone to climb out of the *buraku* because of that. Our new laws make it theoretically illegal for employers, for example, to check up on that sort of thing—but if they're interested, and they are, there are ways. A bribe to a petty official, a private detective—it can be managed."

"So the *burakumin* are stuck?" I asked.

"For now," he said, "but it will change. It's bound

to." He added a bit shamefacedly, "I must admit that even today you will see schoolchildren holding up four fingers when they learn that a classmate is *burakumin*."

Four hundred years does seem an uncommonly long time to hang on to a prejudice based on ancestry, so it's not too surprising that a percentage of the *burakumin* have chosen a more glittering background for themselves by adopting the samurai as fictitious ancestors and becoming *yakuza*. For those who have done it, it must have seemed like the only path out of the ghetto, for in that respect at least, the *yakuza* are democratic. They'll take recruits without asking for a pedigree.

I have been speaking of those *yakuza* who are pure Japanese. There are others who are of Korean or Chinese origin, what the Japanese call *sangokujin*, which means "Third Country people." They represent a sizable hunk of the *yakuza* world, although by no means are they the majority as some defensive Japanese friends told me. They too complain of great discrimination and when they go in for being *yakuza*, they are considered by the Japanese to be the most vicious and bloodthirsty of the lot. Chiefly they have their own gangs, or at least that's how they started out, but at this point in gang history they are often affiliated with purely Japanese gangs on a separate-but-equal basis, and there are individual *sangokujin* who have made it into the ranks of Japanese gangs. Some of Taoka's best friends are Korean, but it wasn't always that way.

"I suppose," said Miyazawa-san, "we're a little xenophobic. Not as much as we used to be, however. We're getting used to you foreigners who come to visit and even stick around to do business, and except for your friends the *yakuza* and a few other segments who cling to traditionalism, we don't really regard you as 'hairy barbarians' anymore."

"Thanks a lot," I said, "but what about the minority groups who live here and who aren't Caucasian? Isn't it true that you give them a pretty rough time?"

He sighed. "That's another matter. You mean the Koreans and the Taiwanese, I suppose."

I did, for I had heard that although many of these had lived in the country for generations, they were always treated as second-class citizens. Not even citizens, but residents, since you don't achieve citizenship in Japan very easily.

"Well," he said, "it's a problem. It stands to reason that those who chose to emigrate were not what you would regard as elite, and it's true we have a great streak of elitism. Coming from a nation of immigrants makes it difficult for you to understand. But to bring it back to your *yakuza,* one of the reasons the *sangokujin* gangs got so powerful was because of you Americans."

I did a large double take on that, and he explained that during the American occupation following World War II, to their delighted surprise, the *sangokujin* suddenly found themselves in the unprecedented position of being teacher's pet, in a way. The Americans trusted them far more than they trusted their recent enemies simply because they were *not* Japanese.

"If I may say so," Miyazawa-san said, "it was a rather naive assumption that they were purer of heart than we were, and they were given access to all kinds of commodities which were in desperately short supply in the country. Food, cigarettes, building materials, clothing. The temptation to cash in on the black market was irresistible."

To say nothing of the temptation to lord it over their former oppressors. Chinese and Korean smuggling and black market combines began to proliferate, using their American-given opportunity not only to get rich, but to get even. The hate they'd been bottling up for so long came spewing out in an orgy of rape and slaughter, most of which was a secret from their American protectors who were too busy trying war criminals to bother with the other kind even if they had been able to recognize them as such. If Kazuo Taoka were a philosopher, he would be grateful for the postwar excesses of the *sangokujin,* for were it not for these, he might never have had the chance to show his mettle and start his climb to fame.

And so these minority groups furnish a sizable number of *yakuza,* but the mother lode still comes from the desperately poor and poorly educated, who have neither the brains nor the equipment to change their status even if the society were to be more hospitable to them. Under the circumstances it is not surprising that they are receptive to the *yakuza,* who seem to offer a way out, a path to riches, excitement and glamor. As in any other business, the number who will achieve these rewards is minimal, for there aren't many Kazuo Taokas around, but perhaps that is not as important to them as the sense of brotherhood and of belonging to something big and powerful.

I cannot leave the subject of Japanese vs. Korean gangster without mentioning that it's not easy to tell the two apart. Not just for me, but for them too. I found that out by answering a summons one day from an American friend who has lived in Japan for more than twenty-five years and has been in a lot of businesses, including cafes, and hence has a broad acquaintance among *yakuza* on all levels, from *oyabun* to lowliest *kobun.*

He was highly amused by my project, and he called me one day at noon with the injunction to get myself right over to an obscure little *sushi* (raw fish) parlor where he was about to have lunch with an old acquaintance whom he had just run into. "You want to meet some real live *yakuza,*" he said, "here's your chance. Pretend you dropped in by accident."

I had one hell of a time finding the place, and the odds against a stray American woman wandering into this out-of-the-way joint "by accident" would be astronomical, but I did as I was told and made it, gasping for breath. My friend was watching for me and he rose with a fake air of surprise and a "Well well well look who's here!" and introduced me to his crop-haired companion, who was named Matsumoto. Matsumoto shrank from me as though I had leprosy, barely acknowledging the introduction, but my friend went into a hard sell in his fluent Japanese, and I heard the words *shinrai dekimasu,* which I recognized as meaning "reliable," so Matsumoto gave in and apparently relaxed. I can't, by the way, guarantee that that is his name, but it was the one given me.

I think I won his confidence by attacking the raw fish with vigor, as I happen to love it, and by knowing how to use my *hashi* (chopsticks), which made me seem less foreign, I suppose. Also, I let it drop that I had been born in Chicago, since I understand that has very exotic overtones to Japanese gangsters, and his response was "Ah! Erietnesu!" I thought it was a Japanese word, but my American friend was thumping the counter with laughter. "That's Elliot Ness he's saying," he told me. "He watches *The Untouchables.*" It got to be very friendly all around, and I finally felt courageous enough to ask about Korean gangsters, and how you can tell them from any other kind.

"Plenty of ways" was the answer which my friend interpreted for me, "but one sure way is to get into a fight. When he drops his kimono from his shoulders, you can see the tattoo. If he is tattooed with skull and crossbones, or severed head dripping blood, he is Korean. If he is tattooed with samurai emblems or chrysanthemums or things of that nature, he is Japanese. No problem."

No problem for him, that is. For me it continued to be a problem, since the likelihood of finding myself doing battle with any *yakuza* seemed small indeed.

CHAPTER 5

IN THE '30s the Yamaguchi-gumi was building itself up under the leadership of the second *oyabun,* twenty-eight-year-old Noboru Yamaguchi. Noboru had a lot more get-up-and-go than his father had had, and the Yamaguchi-gumi was getting to be a name to be reckoned with in Kobe. Noboru was taking on the aura of a movie gang leader instead of just a simple labor goon as his father had been, even to having an inner circle of lieutenants. They were all very tough customers, anxious to curry favor, since they were all bucking for first place in the event that anything should happen to their boss—always a distinct possibility considering the high mortality rate among gangsters. The lieutenants had names like Blue Demon, Red Demon, Big Eyes, Ferocious, just as the fellows I was reading about in the *Chicago Tribune* at the time had names like Frankie "The Undertaker" Yale, Machine-Gun Kelley, Terrible Johnny Torrio and Scarface. I've always supposed that the reason for such nicknames was to strike terror in the hearts of rivals, like war paint on an Indian. Since their foes had the same kind of nicknames and the enemy tribes were similarly painted, you'd think it would all be canceled out, but it certainly had the value of good showmanship.

Our Great Depression had affected the rest of the world, Japan included, and even good boys found it hard to get jobs. Kazuo Taoka, having left his only legitimate job as a lathe worker under a cloud, would hardly be able to furnish references to a new employer even if he could find one, which he had little interest in doing in any case. Instead, he did what came naturally, became a confirmed delinquent, although not yet a bona fide gang member. Not that he wouldn't have liked to have been, but it's not so easy to join a gang. You have to prove yourself first, and aspiring *yakuza* are looked over as carefully as university graduates are by major companies.

Kazuo himself records that he wandered aimlessly around the streets of Kobe, picking fights with other delinquents so that he could practice his finger trick. He didn't give them the full treatment—just enough to cause pain and to intimidate them into acknowledging his superiority. He explains it by saying he was letting off steam, and furthermore he has no qualms about what he did, for he says that most of them were good-for-nothing punks who deserved what they got. I don't know on what basis he draws a distinction between them and himself, but apparently he does. His real motive was to call attention to himself, for he was auditioning for the members of the gang. They had become the closest thing he had ever had to a real family, and he wanted them to adopt him.

They saw and noted, as did the police. He was picked up several times, but nothing much came of these arrests and he was let off with a warning in every case. The Yamaguchi-gumi began to look upon him fondly as a little brother, and he was even given a nice, virile nickname—"The Bear." Occasionally they favored him with jobs as a private guard, or a strong-arm man to handle troublemakers in various of the theaters they controlled—for they had begun to enlarge their activities to include actual control of the theaters instead of merely supplying personnel.

In spite of his close friendship with Hideo Yamaguchi, Taoka had never met the *oyabun*, big brother Noboru. He got his chance one day when he got into a hassle with the house manager of the theater where he was filling in as a guard. It was just a petty misunderstanding, but the Taoka temper got out of control, and he ran amok in the theater in pursuit of the manager, scaring most of the audience and the actors out of their wits. What he had done was definitely taboo. After all, this was a Yamaguchi-gumi-controlled theater, not that of a rival, and before he knew it he was hailed into the presence of the *oyabun*.

If he was frightened by the summons—and he was—believe me, he had every right to be. Running afoul of the *oyabun* is ordinarily not punished with a slap on the

wrist. It would depend, of course, on the nature of the
offense, but the range of punishment could go anywhere from simply bowing your head and making
a humble apology all the way to losing your life. In
between there are such refinements as shaving your
head, or for something somewhat more serious, there
is a *yakuza* ritual which goes like this: sitting on your
haunches, dressed in your ceremonial kimono, you
place a clean square of cloth on the table in front of you,
take your *katana* (a short, mean-looking sword) out of
your belly band, place the little finger of your left hand
on the cloth and proceed to cut it off. You then tie it up
in a silk handkerchief and present it to your *oyabun,* and
you'd better pray that he accepts it and slips it into his
kimono at his breast. If he doesn't, instead of walking
around with nine fingers for the rest of your life, you
probably won't be walking around at all.

Taoka had done nothing to merit such extreme punishment, but he was understandably nervous as he sat
before Noboru waiting for the verdict. Noboru spoke to
him softly: "You are Taoka?" Taoka nodded. "The one
called 'The Bear'?" Taoka looked up in happy surprise.
He was known to the *oyabun,* a recognition not often
accorded struggling young hoods. Noboru looked him
over speculatively and appraised his possibilities, for
stories had indeed reached him of Taoka's aggressive-
ness and of his courage too. He decided that with a little
disciplinary training the young man could develop into
an asset to the Yamaguchi-gumi, if only as an "enforcer." The *oyabun* decided to be lenient with him this
time, and he told him quietly to watch his step in the
future. He also put him in the hands of his most trusted
lieutenant, a man named Furukawa, the one who was

nicknamed Big Eyes, the husband of Noboru's sister.

Taoka had achieved the lowest rung on the ladder—that of *sanshita,* or apprentice. The *yakuza* are set up in the same structure as the mafia, more or less, divided into crime families, with each family having its own godfather up at the top. Under him there is a deputy boss and an inner council. They are the brain trust, and the rest of the members of the family, the *kobun,* are the soldiers who perform the menial chores, furnishing muscle, making collections and the like. At the bottom of the heap are the *sanshita,* who are on twenty-four-hour call to do anything that is demanded of them.

For Taoka, being assigned to Big Eyes was a signal acknowledgment of his possibilities. As the number one deputy to Noboru, Big Eyes would in the ordinary flow of events most likely succeed him as the *oyabun,* and Taoka was willing and eager to please Big Eyes in all respects. It wasn't hard to do, for Big Eyes was a big, good-natured fellow, not particularly colorful or exciting, but completely dependable and fair-minded. To young Taoka, Big Eyes was the father he had never had, and he took great joy in being part of a genuine household. He didn't in the least mind the discipline or the work, performing cheerfully all the tasks assigned to him by Big Eyes and by Mrs. Big Eyes—cleaning, shopping, running errands and standing guard most of the night. Besides, it was not all unrelieved labor. At night there was often time off for himself, evenings when he could hang around with the big boys at gang headquarters where the men were gambling—which had become his favorite pastime.

Gambling. No *yakuza* film would be complete without the obligatory scene in which gamblers in their kimonos are sitting in long lines facing each other. The dealer, often a woman, turns up the pasteboards which are small enough to fit into the palm of a hand, and which are known as *hana-fuda* (flower cards). In a *yakuza* movie somebody usually cheats and is found out, at which point the injured party drops the kimono off his shoulder, revealing his tattoos. This is the traditional invitation to fight, and out come the swords—long or short —and the blood flows. It happens that way in real life too sometimes, for since gambling is illegal, it is run by gangsters. The players are often gangsters too, but there is also the usual run of suckers who think they can beat the odds against the pros, even as you and I at Las Vegas.

They don't gamble for matchsticks in Japan. According to the National Police Agency, which is in charge of coordinating all the anti-*yakuza* activities in the country, gambling is one of the chief sources of income for the gangs, with annual profits going into the billions. Until recently it used to be *the* greatest source, but it has been passed by the amount garnered through the sale of illicit stimulant drugs, a rising and booming business. In addition to gambling with cards, sports who like the action can find themselves a mah-jongh game or lose their shirt on the bicycle or horse races (which are government-run, but where the betting is *yakuza*-controlled). There are even very private clubs where you can go for roulette and other Western-style gambling, provided you know somebody who knows somebody, for the security in such places is very stiff.

It is, however, the *hana-fuda* games which interest me
the most as they are uniquely Japanese, and because I
had heard that the very word *yakuza* was derived from
one of the games played with these cards. They are very
beautiful, and unlike Western playing cards there are
no numbers on them. Just blossoms and mountains and
trees and other wonders of nature, but each card does
have a numeric value which you must memorize. The
game which gave the *yakuza* their name is not unlike
blackjack. *Ya* is a shortened version of the word for
eight, *ku* for nine and *za* for three. Together they add
up to twenty, and if that's what you draw, you lose. I
suppose you could interpret that as being society's way
of saying that the *yakuza* are good-for-nothing losers,
but it isn't just the straight society which calls them that,
but the *yakuza* themselves. They prefer this designation
by far to the one which the police use—*boryokudan,*
which means "violence gangs." It is only in recent
years, as a matter of fact, that *yakuza* has become an
all-inclusive term which takes in all the activities of the
various gangs. Up until then, each gang had its specialty, and those who specialized in gambling were
known as *bakuto.* Most of these rigid lines have broken
down, and the *bakuto* have branched out into other
activities.

I badgered everyone I knew who I was dead sure did
a little gambling from time to time, including my old
friend Jiro Tamiya, to get me to a professional game.
They all refused, naturally. Female, foreign, too rough,
impossible, forget it. Jiro-san, however, did describe to
me the technique for getting a game together. With a
straight face, incidentally, as something he had "heard
about." The games operate like floating crap games,

their locale getting moved around from night to night to avoid raids by the police. There are clubs and restaurants where gamblers hang out waiting for the word. It arrives by a *yakuza* emissary who gives the signal—a finger to his nose, for the word for "flower" is the same as the word for "nose," *hana.*

Months after I had returned to New York, my desire to learn a few *hana-fuda* games unfulfilled, I called Rocky Aoki, the owner of the Benihana chain of restaurants, who I knew had a reputation as a man who loves to gamble. I explained my problem and he put me in touch with his general manager at that time, Allen Saito. I explained my needs, Mr. Saito laughed and said he would see what he could do. A week later my phone rang, and a man's voice said, "I understand you want to learn the *hana-fuda* game. Tonight?"

"Tonight," I agreed, and half an hour later I was sitting on the floor of my bedroom with a strange Japanese gambler from Tokyo, being initiated into the mysteries of the *ya-ku-za* game. I had my own *hana-fuda* deck —a farewell present from a group of Japanese friends, who also gave me a genuine *pachinko* machine to hang on my wall, in lieu of getting their crazy American friend admitted to a professional *hana-fuda* game. It's probably just as well. I lost consistently to my obliging Tokyo visitor.

In the *Asahi Geino,* Taoka tells of his preoccupation with the *hana-fuda* games. He was stimulated by the excitement and atmosphere of being around the tough-talking hoodlums who played in them. It made him feel as though he were *kakko-yosa,* one of the gang. As for the gang, they clearly enjoyed having him around, especially as he was such an easy mark. He gambled for stakes he couldn't afford and he invariably lost—a genuine pigeon. He couldn't figure out why, until one night when he had lost all his money, one of the kindly thugs with whom he had been playing offered to stake him.

Taoka was indignant. "I don't borrow money for gambling," he said, whereupon his friend smiled and put a companionable arm around his shoulder.

"Look, kid," he said, "I like your style and I'm going to tell you something. The point of gambling is to be able to read your opponent without letting him read you. You've gotta learn not to laugh whenever you get a good hand and not to look unhappy when it's bad."

Taoka listened carefully to this advice, took it to heart, went out and got himself a hand mirror and spent hours in front of it, practicing a poker face. He also worked hard at his ability to concentrate and tuned up his sensitivities so that he would be able to anticipate the intentions of other players, and sure enough he stopped losing. Now when he speaks of that early discipline in learning how to gamble, he compares it rather whimsically to a college education. On the academic side it forced him to develop qualities which have made it possible for him to outsmart his enemies at every turn; on the social side he established friendships—as one is supposed to do in college—which would help him in the future. He became intimate with men who were to become his partners in future ventures, although none of them dreamed at the time that they would one day call this very junior apprentice by the title *oyabun*.

All in all, these were happy times for Taoka, even if

they weren't for the rest of Japan. Not only was there an economic depression, there was the Manchurian Incident to keep the country occupied.

The year was 1931, which historians consider to be the turning point in Japan's modern history. Depression had seriously damaged the prestige of the Western democracies, and with the failure of many small businesses and much of the farming population, plus the high tariff policy adopted by the United States, there were large segments of the people who began to call to their leaders to look elsewhere for inspiration in running the country and fulfilling their destiny. Japan felt itself on the defensive against what seemed to be a hostile attitude from the Western powers which were intent on keeping it fenced in as a subject nation. Their salvation, the Japanese felt, lay in prosperity achieved through foreign expansion. It was a time of attempted coup d'etats by the extremist military clique, of the assassination of the Prime Minister, and of an aggressive determination to be the dominant power in East Asia. The groups which were pushing for power argued that it was their defense against extinction as a nation.

But Kazuo Taoka did not live in the world which concerned itself overly with such matters. There is no record which shows that he gave much thought to Japan's destiny at that time, but the matter forced itself upon his consciousness because he was called up for military conscription. He made no attempt to dodge the draft. He would, in fact, have been perfectly amenable to doing a stint in the army, since he had no other regular job and he was as patriotic as the next fellow. To his embarrassed surprise, however, he was exempted because he failed to pass his physical examination. The tough guy of the Yamaguchi-gumi juniors was found to suffer from muscle deficiency.

If Taoka's political philosophy was as yet undefined, this was not true of the budding godfather of the right, Yoshio Kodama. He was deeply concerned with his country's politics, and his ultranationalist point of view was already well formulated. Thus far in their respective careers, all the two had in common were their age and the fact that both had had their woes with the police —Taoka for assorted acts of mayhem, and Kodama for inflammatory right-wing activities, for which he had been imprisoned.

Turned down by the army, Taoka went back to living out his apprenticeship with Big Eyes Furukawa, a period of two years, after which he moved into his own flat, sharing it with a few card-playing buddies who, like himself, had no regular occupation. They were good enough to be occasional card hustlers, strong enough to be occasional bodyguards, and they lived by their wits and muscles, aimless and unconcerned. They hadn't yet made Taoka a regular member of the Yamaguchi-gumi with all the hocus-pocus accompanying ritual, but he had the status of junior and was expected to do whatever the gang demanded of him. He was not only willing, he was eager—sometimes even a bit overzealous.

For instance, one night he was hanging around the stage door of a movie house chewing the fat with his best pal, "Tiger" Yamada. He looked up and to his surprise, he saw a famous figure rushing toward him, a sumo wrestler whom he'd hero-worshipped for quite some time. It was a pretty imposing sight, for sumo wrestlers weigh between two hundred fifty and three

hundred pounds, and the man had his traditional pig-
tail coiled into a top-knot and his kimono sleeves flap-
ping. Taoka was thrilled to actually see him in the flesh.

The wrestler seemed agitated, and he was in the company of a Yamaguchi-gumi senior. He came directly to
Taoka and Yamada, panting, "I have been insulted! I
am asking you to help me to take revenge!" The
Yamaguchi-gumi senior nodded affirmation and explained that it was another wrestler who had tendered
the insult, and the aggrieved party could not take his
own revenge, as he was being considered by the Wrestling Committee for a first-rank status and could not
afford the scandal of a public brawl or worse. Taoka and
Yamada saw it as a golden opportunity to prove their
virility, their courage and their willingness.

Arming themselves, Tiger with a gun and Taoka with
a two-foot long sword, they went with the wrestler to
the hotel of their quarry, breaking into the room to do
battle. Alas, he lay on the floor asleep, drunk and snor-
ing. Taoka was disgusted and frustrated, for the spirit
of adventure demanded an adversary capable of giving
him a fight. He kicked him in the side, shouting, "Get
up, damn you! And apologize for the insult!" The
sleeping beauty opened one eye, saw the wrestler and
two armed thugs, rolled over on his mountainous bulk
and told them to get lost.

The insult to the wrestler was now compounded with
the insult to Taoka, and he reacted with the emotion
which had become an integral part of his personality—
uncontrollable rage. Blinded with fury, he began
smashing at his victim with his sword, until the man he
had come to avenge, appalled at the force he had set
into motion, pleaded with Taoka to stop and begged

the wrestler on the floor to apologize, not only to satisfy the insulted wrestler's pride, but to end the bloodshed.

Taoka was bewildered by this about-face, and he lost control of his movements although he could not make himself stop. His sword slipped, grazing the cheek of the wrestler on the floor and cutting off two of his fingers. He was barely restrained from killing his mutilated and by now thoroughly sober victim who, covered with blood, got to his knees and apologized. Taoka had not put an end to his life, but he had certainly finished off his career. With a gift for understatement, he has said in recounting this incident in his published memoirs that there seemed to be very little demand for wrestlers with eight fingers.

It was not, by the way, in the least strange that a wrestler would come to the Yamaguchi-gumi for help. Wrestling is a big source of income for gangster groups. They control the contracts of most of the wrestlers, are the entrepreneurs who arrange the matches, control a hefty share of the take, the ticket sale both legal and scalped, and the various concessions which surround all popular sporting events are run by gangsters as well. In recent years the Japan Pro-Wrestling Association had as one of its directors Kazuo Taoka, which was what accounted for the miniature tower trophy I saw in his house, but back in the '30s Noboru Yamaguchi had not yet made such strong inroads in the sports world. He was getting there, however, courting the tons of beefy pigtailed wrestlers who are among the country's favorite performers, wining and dining them, doing whatever favors he could in order to put himself into the management picture. He had not given up his waterfront activities, but they did not occupy him to the extent that show business and sports did, both of which were more to his taste. Furthermore, he saw them as a means of expanding his activities and increasing his territory outside of Kobe.

As with the wrestlers, the theaters controlled by the Yamaguchi-gumi could be exploited for profit in many ways, with the illegal revenue from ticket-scalping, the various grafts in the form of kickbacks from tradesmen and artisans and suppliers of equipment, but Noboru was not satisfied with that. He saw a chance to increase his profits immeasurably by controlling the very attractions which played in his theaters.

The most popular entertainers of the day were *rokyoku* singers, who do traditional ballads, singing with native instruments and telling folk tales. The really good ones enjoyed—and still do—the same kind of popularity as the Rolling Stones, for instance, with packed houses, hysterical fans, the works. If you booked such an act into your theater you were assured of stand-up business for the length of the engagement, and the profits from ticket-scalping were really extraordinary, so great was the demand. Noboru Yamaguchi was a first-class salesman, and he made contact with the managers of a number of these singers, acquiring the rights to present them in Kobe as a producer, rather than a theater manager, with the understanding that he would stay out of the territories of other gangsters who had controlling rights elsewhere. Noboru didn't lose any sleep over such "agreements." He was beginning to make a few powerful connections among politicians on a quid pro quo basis, raising money for campaigns (providing the politicians were properly conservative in their politics) and sending his *kobun* around to get the vote out. In return, he was given protection in any territorial disputes which might arise. It was still peanut stuff, confined to places in the vicinity of Kobe, but it was a beginning in the expansionist policy. Noboru was a canny man, but as things developed, he was not in the same league with, nor had he the same vision as, his very junior member Kazuo Taoka, who at that time had not even been initiated into the mysteries of full gangsterism.

Love. Kazuo Taoka had attained the age of twenty-two without ever experiencing the tender, ennobling emotion which makes the world go round. Sex was something else again. He wasn't exactly a matinee idol, but he was not without attractions. That funny cockeyed smile, the sharp intelligent eyes, a slight but powerful build, a quick wit—he could certainly have had all the *suke* he wanted. *Suke* is *yakuza* slang for the kind of girls one finds hanging around gangsters: dice girls, bar girls, hostesses, hookers, the usual run of women who work in something called *mizushobai,* which means literally "water business," and seems an accurate description for the cafes and restaurants where the tab is so high, you seem to pay a premium just for water. But Kazuo Taoka is Japanese, and his ideas concerning marriage were the same as those of other Japanese who are not *yakuza:* his ideal was a "good" woman—chaste, feminine, obedient, devoted to home and family as his own mother had been. The kind of woman, in short, who would drive Gloria Steinem and Betty Friedan and company up the wall.

Although it has become more common for Japanese young women and men to choose their own marriage partners (the changing picture, with women entering the business world more and more, and dating becoming an ordinary event, accounts for that), it is still true by and large that the family will play a major role before anything is definitely decided. The parents of the boy will in all probability examine the girl carefully to see that she has good character, good education, good health so that she can bear children, not unlike buying a mare. They may even hire an investigator from a marriage agency to look into the background of the girl.

But before the war, even the option of choice was not left to the marriage candidates. It follows that no sensible parents would go dancing in the streets at the thought of having a gangster for a son-in-law, especially since Taoka was not even a successful one as yet. Thus, when he laid eyes for the first time on the girl of his dreams, he knew he had a rough road to travel before he could attain his heart's desire.

She was sitting in a little cafe where he had dropped in for a cup of coffee, but she was no cafe hostess. She was the daughter of the owner of the place, and her name was Fumiko Fukayama, a shy, lovely creature with melting eyes. The minute he looked at her, he knew that she was the girl for him, and her hesitant smile and lowered eyes told him she was similarly attracted. There *are* those women who like the big, strong, virile types who make them feel helpless and feminine and who push them around a bit, which may account for the fact that many girls from perfectly respectable, polite backgrounds are attracted to hoods and gunmen. In addition to the hostility of her parents, Taoka faced another obstacle where Fumiko was concerned—she was only fourteen years old at the time, which is pretty young for marriage even in Japan. Just the same, he set his heart on marrying her—and eventually he did—but it took him four years to accomplish this, and one of those years was spent in jail.

Considering the nature of his crime, a one-year sentence was practically a gift from a friendly judge. Taoka had undertaken what amounted to a *kamikaze* mission to avenge the death of one friend and the injury of another at the hands of some merchant seamen in a union dispute. The sailors had demanded an improvement in labor conditions, and Noboru Yamaguchi had been called in—naturally on the side of management. He sent around a pair of "arbitrators" (read strike-breakers) from Yamaguchi-gumi ranks, who arbitrated by attacking the union leaders with knives. The death of one of Taoka's friends and the injury of another were the result of the arbitration, and when the news reached Taoka he set out for union headquarters all alone to take revenge.

Reasonably certain that he would not return from his mission, he could not resist the temptation to stop first at the cafe to say goodbye to little Fumiko. He didn't tell her where he was going, but she saw the grim expression on his face and the outline of the sword under his kimono, and she pleaded with him not to go wherever he was bound for. Even her tears could not stop him, and he took off after formally bidding her farewell as he would have on his deathbed, determined to take as many lives as he could before the opponents took his.

He was no sooner on his way than Fumiko, shaking with fright, ran out of the cafe in the direction of Yamaguchi-gumi haunts to find one of his friends, most of whom she knew only by sight. She found one, and

crying hysterically and babbling incoherently she gestured in the direction she had seen Taoka disappear.
He got the idea, immediately armed himself with an
iron pipe and took off in pursuit. A bloody sight greeted
him when he broke into union headquarters. Taoka,
holding his sword with both hands in front of him,
yakuza fashion, was cutting the air left and right, slashing everyone who tried to get at him. Two dead men lay
on the floor, and many other men were clutching their
wounds and screaming with pain. Taoka was like a man
possessed, and his friend, using every ounce of his
strength, finally succeeded in dragging him away before
the enemy could regroup and figure out a plan to over-
take this madman and kill him, which they surely would
have done considering their numbers.

Taoka and his friend made their escape to the home
of Big Eyes Furukawa, who found Taoka some clothes
and hustled him out of town, to Kyushu. Fumiko, her
face a study in sorrow, came to the station to see him
off, not knowing whether he would ever be allowed to
come back to Kobe, but no sooner had he left than the
inner council of the Yamaguchi-gumi met and made the
decision that he should give himself up to the police. If
this seems like a betrayal, it was actually in keeping with
an old tradition, no longer operative, which went back
to the early nineteenth century, when gangs made their
deals with the police, promising to keep their own il-
legalities within certain limits and even to help the police against rival bands with information, in return for
protection. There may have been a little bit of that left
in the early '30s when all this was happening to Taoka.
Clearly it was for the "good of the gang" to hand over
a murderer to the police rather than to have them step

in and put the heat on the entire organization. Like a good soldier, Taoka did as he was told. In return for his submission to authority, the Yamaguchi-gumi arranged with a criminal lawyer to represent him at court, and the one-year sentence was the result. The police could write "finis" to the incident, the Yamaguchi-gumi could conduct its business without interruption, Taoka could prove his loyalty and everybody was happy. Except, perhaps, Fumiko who went every day to the shrine to pray for his safe return.

Her prayers were answered. With pride, Taoka recounts how he came out of jail a full-fledged hero, met at the gates by top-ranking members of the gang, up to and including Noboru Yamaguchi himself. There was a welcome-home banquet of the kind which is usually reserved for high-ranking seniors and *oyabuns*, held at an expensive restaurant, lots of thank-you-for-taking-the-rap-for-all-of-us speeches, a present of a ceremonial kimono, and Noboru gave him his own, very valuable sword. Hercules had performed all his labors, and now at last he was deemed ready for full membership.

He was still technically pledged to Big Eyes Furukawa, and so Noboru had to follow the protocol of asking Big Eyes for permission to take him over and assume responsibility for him. Big Eyes gave his formal agreement, and so, with a ritual exchange of sake cups and the swearing of oaths not to betray his brothers, to observe the *oyabun-kobun* relationship and never to betray the secrets of the Yamaguchi-gumi, Taoka finally made it into the gang. The year was 1936.

That same year Fumiko's mother had died, and as soon as the proper period of mourning was over, Taoka overrode all the objections of her father and made her his bride. He moved her into a small apartment which they shared with four of his cronies, and she uncomplainingly cooked, cleaned, washed and ironed, picked up after them and listened to them–that is to say, when she was not working in her father's cafe to earn enough money for all of them to live on. Taoka had indeed found a girl just like the girl who married dear old Dad.

CHAPTER 6

THE KIND OF ceremony which Taoka was greeted with when he came out of prison is part of the *yakuza* mystique which continues unabated into the present day. The society is a lot more prosperous today than it was in 1936, and so are the *yakuza*, naturally enough, since the latter feed upon the former. Taoka's reception was pretty good for his day and his stature, but it was nothing compared to the lavish and raucous ceremonies which go on today on such occasions, and which are the despair of the police and the public.

In the summer of '73, for instance, I was up very late

one night, my ears pressed to my little transistor, listening to the Watergate hearings being broadcast live over Armed Forces Radio. The thirteen-hour difference in time had them starting at eleven P.M. Tokyo time, which ruled out sleep a great many nights. The ringing of the telephone broke into John Dean's testimony, and the voice on the other end of the phone was that of an American journalist, who said, "You can't leave Japan without seeing a coming-out party."

"You're not only interrupting history," I said, "but you're crazy! I'm not researching debutantes."

"I'm talking about a coming-out-of-jail party, stupid," he said graciously.

I forgot about John Dean. "When?" I asked.

"Tomorrow morning. I'll pick you up at five-thirty A.M.," he said.

"JESUS!" I replied.

"I know," he said, "but I think you'll find it's worth it. You can always read about Watergate, but you may never see anything like this again."

Promptly at five-thirty he drew up to the Imperial, I wedged myself into his Toyota between him, the cameraman and his equipment and we drove for almost three-quarters of an hour in the dawn's early light to Chiba prison. Our man had not yet emerged from the prison gates, nor would he for another hour, but I saw the wisdom of getting there early. For as far as the eye could see, there were cars and buses which had been arriving in a steady stream, I was told, all night long from every part of Japan, filled with friends and admirers of the internee. There were other journalists and photographers scurrying around, popping their flashbulbs, and there was a handful of curiosity-seekers, but the preponderant number of people who had assembled for the event were *yakuza*.

A double file of junior members were lined up on either side of the prison gates to form a guard of honor, rather like a West Point wedding, but without the swords. They wore *happi*-coats, which are hip-length kimonos, over their suits, and the coats were of identical pattern with the gang insignia emblazoned upon them. Like my own honor guard at Taoka's house, they were crew-cut and wore sunglasses although the sky was a murky gray. Older, more important members were dressed in dark suits and many of them wore armbands, and I read later that there were about a thousand of them milling around, the largest turnout for such an occasion ever recorded. Watching them bitterly were about twenty or thirty policemen dressed in riot regalia, helmets and all, against any possible disorder, but one wonders what they could have done even if they wanted to, considering the wide disparity between their numbers and those of the gangsters. But the gangsters were not armed so far as anyone could tell, and the right of peaceful assembly exists in Japan as it does in our country, so the hands of the police were tied. Who was to say that the members had no right to be there so long as they behaved like ordinary citizens? The police are unhappily aware that the *yakuza* use these occasions, among other purposes, as a public nose-thumbing gesture to demonstrate their power and their solidarity.

In point of fact, the police were not too happy about my presence either. I stood out in that crowd like a sore thumb, although there were other foreigners there who were newsmen, but I was the only woman I could see, and I never felt more like a blue-eyed foreign devil than when a cop who caught sight of me sauntered over to where we were standing and had a few words with my escort. I was all prepared to climb back into the car and pull a scarf over my head, when my friend said, "It's okay. I told him you're from the *New York Times.*" I sent silent apologies to West 43rd Street and produced a guest card from the Foreign Correspondents' Club, waving it nonchalantly and praying that the policeman couldn't read English. I can't say he was thrilled to have me aboard even with my phony credentials, but he had enough problems to worry about and he let it pass. The police are not proud of these occasions and feel frustrated by their incapacity to cope with them—hamstrung, one might say, by these legal niceties such as civil rights. Already under attack by the public and press for not "doing something about it," they could not have been very happy to have a foreign observer watching the scene.

As the prison gates opened, a thunderous roar went up from the welcoming party, and cameras clicked and flashed from all directions. "Who's all this for?" I asked, and my companion said, "Shigemasa Kamoda. *Oyabun* of the Kamoda-gumi. The Kamoda-gumi is an affiliate of the Yamaguchi-gumi, and Kamoda is an important henchman of your chum." (He meant Taoka, of course. I had taken a lot of ribbing on the level of what's-a-nice-Jewish-lady-doing-with-gangsters from him before. I loftily ignored it.)

"How long has he been in jail?" I asked.

"Eleven years," was the reply. "He was put away for killing one man and maiming another with a sword."

I remembered that that was precisely what Taoka had done and that he had only drawn a year sentence and I remarked on it.

"Ah," he said, "but that was in another era when nobody took gangsters all that seriously. Taoka was just a petty hood at the time anyway, not big enough to make a splash in the newspapers to prove that the police were on their toes. Now they're really out after these guys, and Kamoda was a big gun. They had nailed him on an incident in one of those full-scale gang wars. They sentenced about fifty other gang members at the time, but he was the most important and they wanted to make an example of him, so he got the longest sentence." (I'm not entirely sure of the beneficial results of this "example," since in the eleven years that Kamoda had spent in jail, gangster figures had climbed precipitously, and anyway Kamoda's place had obviously been kept warm for him.)

By climbing to the top of the car I got a glimpse of Kamoda as he made his appearance, formally attired in *haori* (knee-length kimono) and *hakama* (sort of a split skirt-like affair, ankle-length, topped by a wide belt over a surplice top). There was a mass bow which he returned, and one by one, senior spokesmen came forward and made speeches, to which he responded. The juniors formed a lane for him as he was escorted to the leading car, and others produced walkie-talkies with which they directed participants into their vehicles for the victory caravan to a nearby hotel where there would be a preliminary celebration, after which the honoree would grab a little rest and they would proceed to Kobe for the special banquet at Yamaguchi-gumi headquarters.

I was back at the hotel by noon, and in the elevator going up to my room I kept repeating to myself, "Kamoda, Kamoda." It was familiar, and I looked through my notes which I had been accumulating. "Got it," I said, "the Blue Castle Incident." It was an episode in Taoka's life which had particularly interested me as a striking example of the maneuvering whereby he had been able to extend his influence from Kobe to include all of Japan. Here, the police version and Taoka's are almost identical.

The gang war to which my journalist friend had alluded had been fought with a powerful Korean gang called the Meiyu-kai, which had its headquarters in Osaka. Osaka is a half-hour bus ride from Kobe, as I recall my own pilgrimage, dangerously close to Yamaguchi-gumi headquarters where Taoka held sway. At the time of the Meiyu-kai war, Taoka was already a powerful *oyabun* with growing influence in the Kansai area and the Meiyu-kai was a thorn in his side, not just because they were also powerful, but because they were Korean. From his point of view they were a contemptible lot. Bullies and thugs, they were given to setting fires, robbing, murdering, causing injury to honest citizens—all of these being activities which traditional *yakuza* profess to eschew. In his memoirs he noted that "they walked with naked bosoms, showing off their tattoo of skull or heads just cut off, and with see-through half-length drawers—not just in their own territories, but all through the city. They threw fear in all citizens." When Taoka says "citizens" he means people who are not gangsters, people who are entitled to respect.

In addition to being the disgusting, ill-bred louts that Taoka describes, there was the very real threat which they posed to the supremacy of the Yamaguchi-gumi in the area. With their subsidiary families, acquired through chopping down other rival gangs, the Meiyu-kai numbered approximately a thousand members, half as many as the Yamaguchi-gumi did at the time, but Taoka was not yet ready for an all-out confrontation with them. There had been some skirmishes between the gangs, and while Taoka was not afraid of them, he had another plan at the time. This was the period in which he was engaged in building legitimate fronts through which his gang could operate. To bring the police down on their heads through bloody gang wars would have been poor operational tactics, yet in spite of his desire to side-step any such major gang war, he was himself the unwitting cause of the beginning of the battle.

It started with a comparatively minor incident. Taoka was in Osaka for the opening of a nightclub called King, which was owned and operated by the boss of a Yamaguchi-gumi affiliate. It was to be a quick visit just to show that poppa cared and to wish luck and give his blessing, for he was scheduled to attend an important conference the next morning in Yokohama. He was important enough to travel now not only with his body-guard, but with a secretary, a man named Joji Oda.

The opening was festive and successful, and every-one wanted to extend the evening a bit by going on to a supper club called The Blue Castle for a midnight snack. They took the star of the show with them, a singer named Yoshio Tabata, and the Yamaguchi-gumi men settled into their ringside tables feeling expansive and convivial. They were on Meiyu-kai turf more or less, in Osaka, and it was not surprising that a good many other tables were occupied by hard-drinking, loud-mouthed Meiyu-kai hoodlums. Joji Oda was not seated with his boss and friends, since it was his job to park the car, and he hadn't been able to find a parking place in the crowded nightclub area—an unfortunate happenstance for Oda. The Taoka party had no sooner finished giving their orders to the waiter when a group of Meiyu-kai men sauntered over to their table with challenging smiles, obviously bent on raising a little hell.

Ignoring the Yamaguchi-gumi men, they addressed themselves to the singer. "Hey there, Tabata," one of them said, "how about a little song? We're great fans of yours, but nobody invited us to your opening. Maybe they didn't think we were important enough." They were either too drunk, or perhaps they really had never seen him before, to recognize Taoka, and when one of his men said, "Watch it! Do you know who you're talking to? This is . . . ," Taoka tugged at his arm and signaled him to be silent. He wanted no part of a nightclub brawl at this stage of his career and so, changing his tone, his companion explained politely that Tabata was very tired and just wanted a quiet bite to eat and a nightcap. Perhaps another time. The Meiyu-kai men were too keyed up to settle for that, however, and they started shoving the singer and the other men at the table. Wishing to protect their *oyabun*, the Yamaguchi-gumi men hustled Taoka out of the club—to be met at the entrance by Oda, who had only just found a parking place. He took in the scene and rushed into the club to enter the fray, by now a free-for-all. Poor Oda did all he could to erase his shame at not having been at his *oyabun*'s side to protect him, but long after the incident was over and done with, he felt he would never live it down, so he resigned from the Yamaguchi-gumi and started his own gang, the Oda-gumi. There were no recriminations.

Taoka had not asked for the incident, but since it had occurred it would have been like sticking his tongue out at opportunity not to have taken advantage of it. To take over the lush Minami territory of Osaka had long been his ambition, and while it is his story that he was sitting quietly in Tokyo during the three weeks of the gang war which ensued, it was certainly done in his name and with his acquiescence and advice. The insult to the *oyabun* was the trigger, and indeed if the Yamaguchi-gumi had *not* sought revenge, they would have earned the scorn of the *yakuza* world. The timing was right too, because the police had already begun to crack down on the Meiyu-kai and it was beginning to crumble around the edges.

The Meiyu-kai executives were none too happy about the incident and they sent an emissary to Yamaguchi-gumi headquarters to see if they could work something out in the way of an apology which would avoid a war. "In what manner do you propose to apologize?" they were asked. "By bowing our heads," was the reply. It was not acceptable, but the Meiyu-kai executives were afraid of anything more emphatic because it might lessen their authority and demoralize their ranks and they made the unhappy decision to fight it out.

In the Taoka memoirs, a Yamaguchi-gumi member has described the strategy which Taoka worked out: "We formed small units with men from other groups whose names we didn't know, so that if the police picked us up, we couldn't even tell them if we wished

to who our companions were. We went looking for
Meiyu-kai people, and if we saw someone who looked
like a Korean, even if he was just a pedestrian, we surrounded him and tore off his shirt. If he was tattooed
with skull and crossbones or with a severed head, we
would stab him with a knife and kill him on the spot. We
did this regardless whether it was day or night."

For two weeks these attack units went everywhere
that Meiyu-kai members and executives were known to
hang out, including the homes of their mistresses. The
final battle was under the leadership of Kamoda. It
ended with his running a sword through the chest of a
top Meiyu-kai executive and through the sides of three
of his principal lieutenants. Seven of the remaining executives arrived at Yamaguchi-gumi headquarters with
the kind of apology they should have offered in the first
place—a box containing seven small glass bottles, in
each of which was a severed little finger. The governing
body of the Yamaguchi-gumi accepted the offering, and
thus ended the incident. It also ended the Meiyu-kai,
whose totally demoralized ranks scattered, and many of
whose executives joined the Yamaguchi-gumi. The territories were now firmly in their control, and gangsters
throughout the Kansai area understood that from that
point on, the Yamaguchi-gumi was the force to reckon
with. The incident brought on an investigation by the
Osaka police and forced the arrest of fifty-seven gangsters and the eleven-year sentence of Kamoda. To
Taoka it was probably a fair exchange for the new territory.

When Kamoda came out of jail, I had asked my journalist friend whether every prisoner rated this kind of

shindig. "Pretty much," he had said. "Not this big, but big enough to drive the local residents crazy. And the police—they take it on the chin from everybody, and on top of everything else they have to take those sneers from the gangsters."

I thought about the mafia, which goes to such lengths to deny its very existence. ("The mafia? What's a mafia?" Joe Columbo had said. "There is no such thing as a mafia.") I remarked that it seemed strange to me that *yakuza* don't seem to mind having people know that they're *yakuza*.

"Mind?" said my friend. "On the contrary. Most of them are proud of it—shows they belong to something. Do you know what it means to be a lone wolf in Japan? It means you're nothing—and I'm not kidding. You ask a guy what he does for a living—he doesn't tell you. He says, 'I work for Mitsubishi,' or wherever he works. It's not so important what he does, it's where he does it. You've got to have a *place* under the Rising Sun. It's what gives you status. Now most of these guys, let's face it, are not great brains to begin with. On their own they'd be losers all the way. This way they can swagger around and kid themselves that they're big shots, part of a powerful army that will back them up if they get into trouble. And an influential father, a guy like Taoka or half a dozen others, beats the fathers they started out with or they wouldn't be here.

"That's another reason why these demonstrations are so important to the boys. Sure, they're public-relations gimmicks thought up at the top, dressed up in all that *giri* and *ninjo* bullshit to make the public believe it's based on the old *bushido* code of the samurai warriors." (The *bushido* code embraces stoic endurance of pain, hunger and imprisonment, and envisions violent death as a tragic, poetic fate.) "But the rank-and-filers who aren't ever going to get anywhere, they need it, all the ceremonies and hoopla. It's all they've got to give them a sense of importance and of belonging to something. And most of them will go along with anything to hang on to that. They're dead without it."

He told me about other public occasions on which the *yakuza* can parade around in their lodge uniforms —the installation of a new *oyabun,* the opening of a new headquarters, the funeral or wedding of a member—all lavish and costly affairs in present-day Japan. "Your chum," he said, "has presided over more banquets than the Prime Minister. Of course, he's been in office longer. He's a very smart cookie, and he instinctively understands the psychological value of the rigmarole."

That he does. As Mitsuru Taoka had told me, "It is not fear which keeps my father's men bound to him. It is love and loyalty for all he has done for them." The biggest thing he has done for them is to give them a sense of belonging. To quote one of Japan's foremost psychologists, Dr. Hiroshi Minami, "Obviously many Japanese youths have turned *yakuza* and joined their *boryokudan* in the process of seeking their emotional stability and sense of security." Taoka knows that without being told. It's the story of his life.

CHAPTER 7

IN 1936, when Taoka was sworn into the Yamaguchi-gumi, money was not so plentiful and his initiation was a modest, though highly emotional affair. However, all that oath-taking and ritual-enacting notwithstanding, the big idea in criminal circles is to make money, even by honest means if absolutely necessary, and every member has the responsibility to contribute his share toward keeping the gang solvent. Now, in his elder-statesman days, Taoka's claim is that he sees his major responsibility to be that of getting every one of his *kobun* a job. That's not just an empty claim. He works at it, and the police record that as one of his major accomplishments.

A job is something he didn't have back there in 1936, and his *oyabun*, Noboru Yamaguchi, thought it high time that he got cracking. Taoka was all rested up from his jail term, the honeymoon was over, and Noboru said to him one day, "Let's see how smart you are. Why don't you see if you can arrange a *hana-kogyo?*" A *hana-kogyo* is a particularly risky show business venture (although if anyone knows of such a thing as an unrisky show business venture, I wish they'd tell *me* about it so I can tell my husband). The words mean "flower presentation," but no flowers are involved. Just an entertainer.

What makes a *hana-kogyo* especially venturesome is that it entails a maximum outlay of funds with a minimal return on the investment for the entrepreneur. The only reason to do it is to increase one's prestige in show business. You get yourself a hit with a big star, who probably gets most of the profits, but you build yourself a reputation which makes it easier for you to get the next show and to get somewhat better terms for yourself. Anyway, Taoka had to round up the artist, guarantee his salary, the cost of the theater, the printing of tickets and whatever promotion was necessary. For his pains he would receive only a small share of the profits, for they had to be divided with the artist's personal manager. But at twenty-four, his age at the time, all things seemed possible, and although he realized he could lose his shirt, that risk seemed less than the one of inviting the scorn of his *oyabun* for lacking courage.

It is knowing how to promote that separates the

sheep from the goats in show business, and Taoka exhibited a natural talent for this. First he fast-talked the
manager of a popular *rokyoku* singer into letting him
present his artist in Kobe, then he managed to con
money out of every bartender, hostess and brothel-
keeper in town. They accounted for half of his capital.
The other half came from his wife, who wouldn't tell
him where she got it, but he suspected that she had
borrowed it from her father.

Fortunately for his future credit rating, he did manage to pull the show off. He didn't get rich, but it raised
his stature with his *oyabun,* and it had another long-
lasting effect, that of giving him a taste for and a lifelong
love affair with show business people. In return, they
have certainly contributed to his prosperity. (I am personally happy that he had such a success with his first
venture, because I think my own connection with the
theater played a part in his decision to let me come
calling on him. "I am always happy to be of service to
people in the theater," he had told me, "when they
need my advice or backing or whatever else I am capable of giving them. I feel much *giri* toward all people of
the entertainment world." I was glad of my credentials,
even though I had achieved them through marriage
rather than through direct participation.)

In this aspect of his career, by the way, Taoka developed a talent for picking winners which any Broadway
producer would envy. Ten years after that first small
sortie into show business, a gangly thirteen-year-old
girl, the daughter of a poor Yokohama fishmonger, was
singing in an amateur contest in a bombed-out concert
hall. She was brought to Taoka's attention, and when
he heard her, he took over her management and be-

came a surrogate father to her. He bought her a wardrobe, saw that she got some professional training, forced her on the attention of managers of theaters (who by then listened most attentively when Taoka spoke), and dictated not only her career but her private life and behavior.

Her name is Hibari Misora, and she rates today as *the* top singer in Japan, with a palatial house in Yokohama, an apartment in Tokyo, foreign cars, a star's wardrobe and an adoring public. Before she had achieved her status, when Miss Misora traveled, it was Taoka who was photographed standing behind her and her mother; when Miss Misora was banqueted, it was Taoka who sat at her right; when Miss Misora got married, it was Taoka in striped trousers and cutaway coat who gave the bride away. I don't know what happened to the poor fishmonger.

It hasn't all been caviar and champagne for Miss Misora, however. Among her problems is a notorious brother, whose hero-worship of his sister's protector led him into being a lieutenant of a gang affiliated with the Yamaguchi-gumi. If he were to stick to just gangster activities, it would have no effect on Miss Misora's career—we can't, after all, pick our relatives—but unfortunately this gangster happens to be a terrible ham. He loves appearing up there on the stage with his famous sister, for he fancies himself a bit of a singer himself, and plays the drums too, and Miss Misora has indulged him in his fantasy by insisting that he is an indispensable part of her act. She has discovered, however, that there are limits to the loyalty she can demand of her fans, for they raised such a cry of public indignation that she was banned from appearing in civic auditoriums.

Just for that, she said in an interview with the press, she would appear *nowhere* in Japan for a year. The entire affair, she said, was totally undemocratic, for even if her brother *were* a gangster, which she denied, he was nevertheless entitled to his civil rights and to appear anywhere he wished.

Her denials of his gangsterism rang a little hollow, since the brother has a string of arrests for assault, gambling and illegal possession of weapons. One of the gambling raids in which he was picked up, incidentally, was in big sister's house. And oh yes, I almost forgot to mention—as Taoka is no longer up to active management of his famous protégée, guess who looks after her interests currently? Right. Mitsuru Taoka.

As a young hustler in show business, Taoka did not behave too differently from his legitimate counterparts. Of the more violent aspects of his life, he speaks with a candor which would put a mafia godfather in shock of the youthful high jinks which landed him in jail again after that initial one-year sentence. The facts of that arrest are contained in the voluminous dossier which the police have compiled, but Taoka, in his memoirs, has added a few embellishments, and of course, a great deal of self-justification. To the police one murder may be just like another, but in the *yakuza* world the code of behavior dictates that under certain circumstances the real crime is a failure to commit murder.

It started with a man who was a thoroughly bad hat, in Taoka's opinion, an expelled Yamaguchi-gumi member who was so short on *giri* that he sank low enough to rob the till of the gang. Taoka undertook to rout him out, which he did via an iron kettle filled with boiling

water with which he split his skull. It was a righteous
end, everybody thought. Well, not quite everybody.
The brother of the deceased did not share in the celebration, and he came looking for Taoka at Yamaguchi-
gumi headquarters. Taoka was not surprised to see
him; he had rather expected him since eye-for-an-eye
justice would be a normal expectation. Thus he was
prepared with his long sword, with which he had grown
very skillful, and he ran it through his attacker. Ironi-
cally, this actually could be argued as self-defense, but
by now Taoka's reputation for violence was so well
established that in spite of everything learned counsel
could do, the court decided that he should be put away
for a long time, and he was given an eight-year sentence. To his fellow *yakuza*, The Bear had only succeeded in burnishing his reputation, and while eight
years was a long time to wait, Taoka knew that when he
came out he could count on having an upper-echelon
executive job in the Yamaguchi-gumi. What he didn't
realize in 1936, when all this happened, was that the
Japan he would be coming back to would be very different from the one he was leaving.

By 1937 Japan had blundered its way into an impov-
erishing war with China, and the country's resources
were poured into support of its military machine. The
more moderate elements in the land were silenced, and
belts were tightened to bolster the belief in Japan's
manifest destiny as the dominant power of the Far East.
These events affected the *yakuza* world directly, for like
all other able-bodied men, they were part of the general
mobilization. The gangs began breaking up as the
members became *kobun* of the Emperor.

Taoka, hearing about all this in his cell in Kochi prison, began to think about matters of a political nature for the first time. He suddenly became interested in reading, and he had plenty of time to do it. The books which interested him most were those written by a supernationalist Buddhist philosopher who advocated a return to traditional values, and the biography of a political leader named Mitsuru Kashirayama, who wrote from an extremist right-wing point of view, and who had been one of the early advocates of Japan's attempt to dominate China. Taoka was so impressed with the character of this man that he determined that if he should ever be blessed with a son, he would name him Mitsuru. (From what I saw of Mitsuru Taoka, I doubt that he has in mind dominating anything but the movie business, and if he has inherited his old man's genius for organization, I shouldn't be a bit surprised if he pulls that off.)

Getting to be a political ultraconservative was right in line with *yakuza* tradition, and come to think of it, I don't recall ever having heard of any raving bolsheviks in the ranks of the mafia either. Every social upheaval in Japan's history has found the *yakuza* rooting for the entrenched power, seeking to preserve the status quo. It makes sense. They've made their deals with higher-ups already, and social reformers who come on strong with ideas of a more equitable distribution of wealth, with the inevitable routing out of chicanery and corruption, are anathema to those who want these things to continue. Occasionally there have been struggles between opposing forces for power where the *yakuza* played both sides of the street, but in such cases there

was no real social progress in question—it was only a
matter of exchanging one set of rulers for another. The
same ball game with different players.

There is a disenchanted *yakuza* drop-out, named Koji
Kata, who has written a book dealing partly with the
political outlook of his former brothers. He notes with
irony that *yakuza* and socialists are really warring brothers, born of the same mother whose name is Poverty.
The difference between them, he says, is a character
flaw which sends *yakuza* into the underground of the
establishment to bolster it up when it seems in need,
instead of up on the barricades fighting it where, in his
view, they belong. The flaw, he says, is that they are
essentially lazy and pleasure-loving, that they want to
make that big score and swagger around showing what
big important tough guys they are. On that point he is
at one with Vincent Teresa, who wrote in his book *My
Life in the Mafia:*

> There's one thing everyone should understand about
> mob members. Most of them like to be in the lime-
> light. They like to get all dressed up and go into a
> fancy place with a broad on their arm and show off.
> Ninety percent of all mob guys come from poverty.
> They grew up with holes in their pants, no shoes on
> their feet. They had rats in their room and they had
> to fight for a scrap of bread to eat. Now they made
> it. They got money, five-hundred-buck silk suits, hun-
> dred-buck shoes, ten-grand cars, and a roll of bills
> big enough to choke a horse. It doesn't do any good
> to just look at it. They want everyone to know they've
> made it.

While few grow up to be Taokas, they can dream about it, and Kata's conclusion is that they are supported by cynical elements inside the establishment—politicians, big business moguls, the landed and privileged gentry who recognize the mobs' potential usefulness in protecting their vested interests, and who actually bolster them up with funds and help them to avoid punishment when the occasion demands. When they do get together with the *yakuza* openly, they do it in the name of patriotism.

Taoka's political orientation began taking shape in jail, and Pearl Harbor and the ensuing war with the United States found him dividing his time worrying equally about what would become of the Yamaguchi-gumi and what would become of Japan. The draft, bombs and guns were taking their toll of his old gang, and the ranks of all the other gangs were also being decimated. The *yakuza*, those who were not in jail, were drafted along with everyone else, and where there had been a few dozen gangs in Kobe with a total membership in the thousands, now there were only eight left, and the combined membership had dwindled to less than five hundred men who were draft-proof for one reason or other. A particular blow was the news that his beloved *oyabun*, Noboru Yamaguchi, had died—although not in an air raid or at the hands of an enemy soldier—but as a result of wounds received at the hands of an enemy gangster. Taoka feared that without a strong leader the Yamaguchi-gumi would disintegrate, and he was almost right.

He came out of jail in 1943 while battles were raging all around the world. There was no great coming-out party for him this time. Just a few old friends, some of them in uniform, and of course Fumiko—with whom he had spent only one of the almost eight years they had been married. The hard labor in jail had undoubtedly improved his muscle tone, but since he was disenfranchised as a convicted criminal, he was once again exempted from military service, and after settling into the tiny house which Fumiko had rented in his absence, he returned to his old haunts and his favorite pastime, gambling. In the war-is-hell department, even that had changed, for with enforced blackouts the gamblers had to do all their playing in the afternoon. As usual, patient Fumiko cleaned, swept, picked up after, fed and supported the lot of them.

In all, there were probably twenty or twenty-five Yamaguchi-gumi men still around Kobe on the day that the Emperor's voice came over the radio "opening a path to eternal peace" by accepting the conditions of the Potsdam Declaration. Quite a few of these members were sitting on the floor of Taoka's house playing with flower cards when they heard the news, and without a word each got up and left the house. In spite of the bombs which had made a shambles of Kobe, in spite of the havoc and destruction, and the horror of Hiroshima, they had continued to have a blind faith in the invincibility of Japan. Or perhaps not quite that. They could believe in total destruction. What they could not believe was surrender. Now, however, they must bear the unbearable, endure the unendurable, as their Emperor had enjoined them to do. Taoka too was depressed, but it was at this point that the difference between him and his brothers came to the fore. Where they felt hopeless, he felt challenged. He became a man with a mission. Japan would be rebuilt, and he, Taoka, would rebuild the Yamaguchi-gumi.

To fully understand the miracle which Taoka accomplished, keep in mind that figure of twenty-five members of the Yamaguchi-gumi in 1943. In 1973 a research report done by the National Police Agency listed what they call the Big Seven, the biggest mobs of Japan, and lo, the Yamaguchi-gumi led all the rest with a membership, according to them, of 10,330—a figure which makes Taoka smile condescendingly. This police figure does not take into consideration a newish affiliation with the Inagawa-kai, a Tokyo-based organization which is to the Kanto area what the Yamaguchi-gumi is to the Kansai, and which brings even the official total of men committed to Taoka up to over 20,000. The same report gives the Yamaguchi-gumi the lion's share of earnings of all mobs, garnering through their resources something in the neighborhood of five billion yen, which is a nice neighborhood, but that's only the amount the police can account for. They add disconsolately that in all probability the figure is a lot closer to a hundred times that amount in hidden income.

At the end of the war, however, a new gangster elite was rising in Japan, the *sangokujin*. The members were Korean and Chinese mobsters who, as has been noted, had the unwitting collaboration of the U.S. occupation forces because they were not Japanese. They were growing fat and rich on the commodities to which they had access because of their favored position, and they were growing arrogant because there was no one to call a halt. The police force was inadequate to cope with them, having been divested of much of their authority by the U.S. forces; the demoralized population cowered in fear before them, and certainly the leaderless, tiny group of vagrants called the Yamaguchi-gumi was not equal to the task. War had created devastation—cities reduced to rubble, death and destruction wherever one looked—but peace had added to the sheer physical woes of hunger and disease by leaving the people spiritless, depressed and disillusioned. A people conditioned to trust in the infallibility of their leaders had been left in a state of shock as they now witnessed these same leaders in a position of subservience to the authority of the conquerors.

It was in this general atmosphere that Taoka roamed the streets of Kobe, his hands knotted into fists and thrust into his pockets, his shoulders hunched over, nursing his hatred against the only people who seemed to be prospering in his beloved and shattered country —the *sangokujin*—whom he thought of as mongrels and curs. He fed his resentment by visiting the sites of old haunts which no longer existed: the cinema where he had hung around trading quips with Tiger Yamada, now just a pile of bombed-out rubble; the house of Big Eyes Furukawa where he had spent those happy apprentice years as a *yakuza* junior, razed by B-29s in a raid which had also taken the lives of Big Eyes and his family. Even the headquarters of the Yamaguchi-gumi, once so promising as the seat of a growing authority where he had taken the life of the man who had come to take his—this too was gone.

Taoka's memoirs describe the incident which he considers to have put an end to his restlessness. It happened in the course of one of these aimless, pointless excursions. He was stopped dead in his tracks by the screams of a woman and the cries of a child coming to him from behind a nearby building. He ran toward the sound and saw to his horror a woman being raped by a group of jeering Koreans as her child stood by weeping hysterically. It was the outlet for his rage that he had been searching for. Without stopping to consider that he was outnumbered four to one, he seized the man who was on the ground—it was his turn with the woman —pulled him up, and with the speed of lightning his educated fingers found their target in the eyes of the rapist. Before his victim could even hit the ground, Taoka had seized another and done the same thing, and the other two turned tail and ran from the wrath of this possessed madman, dropping a pistol and an iron pipe as they fled. Taoka knelt at the side of the woman, but her vacant eyes told him that she was catatonic and he knew he could do nothing for her. He tried to soothe the child, patting her and telling her to run and find a policeman, after which he pocketed the pistol and left the scene. For the first time in eight years he felt that old surge of power and exultation. The Bear was on the prowl again.

He had a cause now. With his new-found energy and reawakened sense of being alive, he started rounding up the stray remnants of the Yamaguchi-gumi. With a crusader's zeal he harangued them by the hour, rousing them from their listlessness to his mission, that of ridding the city of *sangokujin*. He attracted new, younger men to his cause. Some were demobilized soldiers who had returned to find they no longer had a place to come back to, others who had been too young for service but whose homes and families had been destroyed and who now roamed the streets foraging for food. Taoka had

become a leader, capable of instilling fire in this unlikely assemblage of vagrants, and they followed him
with an awakened sense of bravado into the black market areas where the *sangokujin* were chiefly to be found.
There was no master plan. Just instructions to provoke
as many fights as possible and inflict as much punishment as they could, using whatever weapons they could
lay hands on. It was hit-and-run, but highly motivated
as they were, they did more damage than was done to
them.

Fighting the *sangokujin* fulfilled all of Taoka's inner
need for violent action, and fortunately the times provided him with great moral justification. It was only
natural that the men who surrounded him fighting at
his side should await his initiative and look to him for
decisions. As a matter of course, they began to call him
oyabun, although there had been no formal decision or
ceremony to justify it. Among the older members, a
Yamaguchi-gumi Brothers Committee had been
formed which functioned in a desultory way as the executive group, but by silent consent Taoka was its head,
and those members to whom he felt closest constituted
the inner circle. They were men he had known before
the war, men like Yuji Yoshikawa, a big burly fellow who
had also been a longshoreman, who had been trained
in Kendo fighting, and who carried a few hand grenades
with him wherever he went.

Yoshikawa was always to be found at Taoka's side. He
was bigger and stronger than Taoka, but it was Taoka's
brain which dictated the strategy of their marauding
expeditions, and it would embarrass Yoshikawa sometimes to be mistaken for the leader. For example, when
the two of them came to the rescue of two young Japa-

nese hoodlums who had been set upon by a group of *sangokujin*, Taoka and Yoshikawa dispersed the enemy, and when the fighting was over, the Japanese introduced themselves and asked the names of their benefactors. Yoshikawa said, "Taoka of Yamaguchi-gumi," and they took it for granted that the bigger, more dignified-looking man was referring to himself.

"We offer you our hands, *oyabun*," they said, and Yoshikawa blushed and said, "Don't call me *oyabun*. *Oyabun* is him!"

These two Yamaguchi-gumi valiants plus their hand grenades were more than a match for sizable groups of *sangokujin*, and Taoka enjoyed challenging them—particularly in places they had taken over which had formerly been Yamaguchi-gumi *nawabari*. Gambling places, for example. Taoka, with his terrific instinct for drama, would break in, sword in hand, with Yoshikawa just behind him holding up a grenade.

"No more gambling!" he would shout. "I, Taoka, say 'no' to you. Out of this place and don't come back!"

As their reputation for violence was well known, everyone present was prepared to accept that they had every intention of using their weapons without thought for their own lives, and it was enough to break up the game and send the *sangokujin* scattering.

Taoka tells how Yoshikawa, before they started on these raids, would say, "*Oyabun*, when we die, we die together. But I want to take as many *sangokujin* with us as possible. It is better than to go to hell with nobody but *oyabun*."

With more and more recruits rallying to their side because of their successes in these ventures, the Yamaguchi-gumi began to rebuild itself, and Taoka became number one on the most-wanted list of the *san-gokujin*. Not only did they put a price on his head, one Korean gang sent him an invitation, or rather a dare, to come calling on them at their headquarters. It was a sneering challenge, of course, and Taoka was aware that he wasn't being asked to tea. Smiling, he passed the letter over to his friend Yoshikawa, who read it, nodded and said, "Sounds very interesting." Taoka debated how many men he should take with him, for it never even occurred to him not to accept the challenge, and then he decided that it would be a distinct psychological advantage to appear with only Yoshikawa, since it would demonstrate how much disdain he had for them.

As he entered their headquarters, arrogantly smiling at the assembled group as though he were backed by an army, he said, "I am Taoka of Yamaguchi-gumi. You wanted to see me, I believe, and I would like to talk to somebody." He added, his voice dripping with contempt, "If there is anybody here who *can* talk, of course. Not your gibberish, but Japanese."

They shouted something in Korean and began to inch their way toward him. He held his knife tightly in his hand, trembling inwardly with more excitement than fear, for he was quite prepared for the possibility that he would die.

Before the fight got started, however, a man burst into the room, said something in Korean, and the would-be attackers fell back. Addressing himself to Taoka he said in Japanese, "Please excuse us. My name is Bonno, and I will make my formal excuses later, but for now do me the kindness to leave here today." Taoka was astonished, but he recognized the name of Bonno and the unusual urgency of his tone, so he decided to go along with him and he signaled Yoshikawa to follow him out.

Bonno, a Japanese himself, was a man with international connections. He had preferred to work with the Koreans rather than try to eliminate them, and he had his own gang, about forty members, who often collaborated with the *sangokujin*. Still, Taoka's reputation had begun to grow, and the Yamaguchi-gumi had begun to make itself felt again, and Bonno would have preferred to be allied with his own kind. When word had reached him that a confrontation was to take place, he had gone to save Taoka's life and to pledge himself and his men to cooperation with the Yamaguchi-gumi. His real name was Masao Sugaya—the name of Bonno, which means "all the desires of life" when written in Chinese characters, having been given him by a Buddhist priest. Taoka never forgets a friend, and as of today Bonno is a chief deputy of the Yamaguchi-gumi and bears still another name, Nakagashira. (It is not unheard of for a Japanese to change his name to fit a new set of circumstances in his life. The actress who played Scarlett O'Hara in the musical was named Sakura Jinguji, but previously, as a part of the Takarazuka company, she had had another name. When she left them to enter a new phase in her career, she changed her name.)

To aid them in their war against the *sangokujin*, the Yamaguchi-gumi found themselves in the unaccustomed position of having some very respectable allies: the police and a cheering public. Not that either group had much practical value, for the police were themselves in the position of being victims. A police lieutenant in Kobe had been abducted and murdered. Another in Suma had been shot to death. A small army of some three hundred *sangokujin* raided a police station, taking some officers as hostages and occupying the telephone communication center. According to Taoka, they planned to take over all the police stations of Kobe to show the Japanese people who was boss.

As a result, the frightened town authority, who served as mayor and chief of police, approached Taoka for help. Taoka was revolted by the decline of dignity on the part of the police which would result in their asking for help from gangsters, but he agreed to help to the best of his ability.

In the Taoka chronicles, a member of a gang called the Sasaki-gumi, which is a spin-off of the Yamaguchi-gumi and closely allied to it, recalls the days of this strange police-*yakuza* detente: "One time we formed a vigilante committee to safeguard a police station. A number of us held the fort while the police escaped through a rear exit with documents which were important to them and which the *sangokujin* wished to destroy. We waited for them to attack, and we dropped hand-made explosives from the top of the building. When they started to scatter we attacked them with swords and whatever guns we could get hold of. The police were very grateful, and they gave us all sake and promised prizes for every *sangokujin* we would destroy! Not only that, they promised they would help us if we came into legal difficulty."

The police have come a long way since those castrated days in postwar Japan, and the tenuous truce between them and the *yakuza* has long since ended. Their fame as crime fighters is worldwide, and they are cited as examples to metropolitan governments in cities everywhere as an exceptionally able and incorruptible body of men. The *yakuza* know they cannot look to them for protection, and their vigorous roundups of gangsters make headlines even in the United States. SIX THOUSAND GANGSTERS ARRESTED BY TOKYO POLICE was the last one I read, in the *Los Angeles Times* in June of 1974. But the short sentences for which the police cannot be blamed are a continuing fact of life in Japan, and even if all six thousand of this group were to be convicted, most of them would be back in business in a year or two. God knows the police try, and the *yakuza* are the first to admit it. Not without grudging respect for their efforts too. At least from some of them.

I spoke with a former *oyabun* who gave up his career as a gangster when he found himself stage-struck and decided to make a stab at show business. He exhibited a great amount of talent, and as of today he is one of the most famous and busy movie producers around Japan. His relationship with his former cronies and *kobun* is amiable, but he has become very respectful of his former enemies, the police. The subject came up when he told me about a script which had been offered to him for production, one which dealt with *yakuza*. Naturally he gets many such offers, considering his expertise, and sometimes he does them. This particular script, though, was such a bloody adventure story, with so many legs and heads getting chopped off in every scene, that he felt he must decline to do it.

"If it had been laid in a different period," he said, "I might have considered it. It was a pretty good yarn. But it's supposed to take place today, and they're going to show this one all over the world, so how would it make us look? Like a lawless people with no respect for au-

thority. The people around the world would get the
idea that these things are a common occurrence in Japan and that they go on without any interference from
the police. That's just not so. Our police are pretty
damned good, you know." And so they are.

But before they got that good, the *sangokujin* had a
picnic making monkeys of them, not just in Kobe but in
all the major cities of Japan, taking over the rackets
which had been the province of the Japanese *yakuza*
with a vengeance, plus breaking up stores and offices
for the sheer pleasure of wreaking destruction on their
Japanese proprietors, attacking people in the streets—
in short, practicing violence on ordinary citizens in a
way no Japanese *yakuza* would have dreamed of in prewar days.

In Tokyo the *yakuza* were experiencing the same re-
naissance of spirit which Taoka had engendered in
Kobe, with old groups reforming into new alliances to
make themselves stronger in order to fight the *sangokujin*. One such alliance called themselves the Ginza Police as an ironic twist, and staked out the Ginza as their
territory from which they would drive out or subordi-
nate the *sangokujin* gangs. They were certainly more
powerful than the actual police, and had more know-
how and greater striking capacity for dealing with the
Third Country gangsters. Old rivalries were temporarily put in abeyance in the practical need to stand together against the intruders, and when territories which
had been previously bitterly fought over in the prewar
days were threatened by the Koreans, it was not uncommon to call on old enemies for support in fighting the
common menace.

One must assume that the American occupation

forces were unaware of these underworld matters during this period. How else can one account for the fact that a massed army of *sangokujin* assembled openly in the space in front of the Emperor's Palace in anticipation of a full-scale gang war with local Tokyo gangsters, armed to the teeth with guns and swords? Again, the police were helpless, deliberately weakened by American policy which took the view that a strong, organized, armed force of Japanese was not to be trusted, and that they could just as well turn against the occupation forces as against their own criminals. The troops on the Emperor's lawn, so to speak, were the boldest display to date of the growing power of the *sangokujin,* and the Tokyo police sent a frantic SOS to the American military police, which arrived speedily and dealt with the situation. It also sent them back to headquarters to rethink their position of permissiveness toward the Koreans, and a new policy was instituted which strengthened the Japanese police, at least sufficiently to enable them to cope with more authority where gangsters were concerned.

There was no question of the attitude of the general public toward the *yakuza* during this period. They looked upon them as heroes and often as saviors, and it is this attitude which bedevils the police even today, for it is hard to erase those memories from the minds of the people who suffered through the postwar chaos and violence of Japan. The *yakuza* were, after all, one of the few symbols of virility on the premises. Emperor, army, navy, police had all been beaten to their knees, they were an occupied country, and only the gangsters in the major cities seemed to have any spirit left in them. The *yakuza* have done their shrewd best to perpetuate this memory.

In addition to fighting the *sangokujin*, Taoka was formulating plans for the future. He had started to think along broader lines than gambling and hooliganism, for he was feeling the heady power of being a leader, albeit an unofficial one. The hero worship he had aroused among younger *yakuza*, who, without being asked, would stand guard at his living quarters armed with swords, touched him deeply. These unsolicited demonstrations of concern for his safety made him understand the true meaning of *giri*, and he began to develop a real sense of responsibility toward his earnest young followers.

In them, he felt, lay the future of the Yamaguchi-gumi, but if the future was to be strong, it would have to have a firmer foundation than the hit-or-miss rackets along the waterfront or gambling. Every member, he felt, would serve the gang better if he were regularly employed, and it would be the first order of business for the Yamaguchi-gumi to see that each had such employment. "As Japan is being newly born," he said at the time, "so must the world of *yakuza* have a rebirth. I, Taoka, solemnly swear to see to it." He voiced these sentiments to the other senior council members, and they responded to this emotional statement by formally asking him to become their *oyabun*. He felt humble, but not so humble that he turned it down. He was thirty-four years old, the first *oyabun* of the Yamaguchi-gumi not in the direct blood line, when he took his oath in

October 1946 at a ceremony held at the Emmeikan, a traditional restaurant in Suma.

They go in for a lot of fancy folderol these days at *oyabun* installations. They are extravagant affairs with a tremendous turnout from affiliate gangster groups all over the country, and in addition to the ceremonial rites there is lots of nonstop drinking and eating which is apt to start early in the morning and continue straight through the day and night. There was one like that in the summer of '73 which infuriated everyone in Tokyo and brought out a spate of newspaper editorials inveighing against the arrogance of the gangsters and the inability of the police to deal with the situation. The *yakuza* had taken over a huge restaurant in the Ueno district, put their men out on the street to redirect traffic away from the place, and wouldn't allow pedestrians anywhere in the neighborhood.

Back there in 1946 when Taoka got installed, money was in short supply and there weren't that many *yakuza* anyway, so it was a modest affair. He's very annoyed, in fact, that the police have represented the occasion as having been elaborate. "They make it sound," he says in his memoirs, "as though we were *tekiya.*" *Tekiya* is a designation for a special kind of gangster, one not very high on the social ladder. The *tekiya* function as street-stall operators, hustlers and con men in the booths which spring up at fairs and shrine festivals and which are year-round features in various neighborhoods. It may not sound like much, but there are hundreds and hundreds of such gangs of *tekiya* around Japan, and the *tekiya* bosses who control their activities have, many of them, become quite powerful. Some have gotten rich enough to build their own hotels, supermarkets, *pa-chinko* parlors, bars and cabarets, and they have made their influence felt in political circles as well. In this way they are similar to mafia groups which have put pressure on certain corrupt politicians in America, backing them with funds and demonstrations on their behalf in return for influence and protection. My friend Tamiya-san took me by a newly opened *pachinko* parlor one evening and pointed out the huge floral wreath in front of it, which was hung with strips of calligraphy. "What does it say?" I asked him.

"Something like you would say, 'Good wishes from your pal so-and-so.' "

"Who's so-and-so?" I asked.

"Local big shot, a politician. This place is owned by a *tekiya* boss who is friendly to this politician, and this wreath, it's a way of saying to other *yakuza*, 'Keep off this territory. We are protected.' " (So it shouldn't be a total loss, we went in and played *pachinko* for an hour. I won a box of candy.)

Unlike our politicians, there are those in Japan who boast quite openly of their *tekiya* connections. One member of the Diet told a researcher of having called on a loyal right-wing *tekiya* boss to organize as many groups as possible to offset a counterdemonstration when he was trying to get a repressive bill through. "The left-wingers were opposing it," he said, "but they didn't dare do anything when they saw the *tekiya* standing three deep around the building. We got the bill through." So their usefulness goes beyond hustling suckers. A sort of interesting sidelight is that the *tekiya*, who have been around for centuries, are said to be named from the two words meaning "arrow" and "mark," and that the "mark" has the same significance as it does with our own confidence men.

At any rate, Taoka is miffed at having his ceremony described as though it were a *tekiya* installation. There is a certain carnival quality associated with *tekiya*, and Taoka says, "We don't slit our wrists and lick one another's blood. That's all *tekiya* foolishness."

Certain traditions were, of course, observed. The exchange of sake cups, for example, which follows a rigid formula: a go-between will do the pouring, and if the exchangees are on an equal basis, each will drink half of what is in his cup before they make the exchange. If a senior drinks with a junior, the senior drinks only forty percent and gives the junior the rest. If a junior drinks with his *oyabun*, he's in clover, for the *oyabun* will drink only thirty percent and give him the rest. It symbolizes everyone's exact standing in the hierarchy, and also says that the seniors are looking out for the juniors.

The cast of characters at Taoka's installation included one ringer, a man named Ryoichi Tsukuda. I mention him only because his presence at the installation of a gangster boss would be the equivalent of, say, the Secretary of Commerce showing up at Carlo Gambino's headquarters when he took over as the head of his "family." Tsukuda was not a member of the Yamaguchi-gumi. What he *was* a member of was the Diet, an official of the Liberal-Democratic Party (LDP); he added his luster to the occasion in memory of his late friend Noboru Yamaguchi, with whom he had had a warm relationship. Tsukuda himself stamped the Taoka ascension kosher by being the one to present him with the emblems of his office: a flag with the Yamaguchi-gumi insignia embroidered on it, a roll of silk, a traditional scroll of blank white paper and a sword. Nobody tried to make a secret of Tsukuda's presence, nor was there a sweeping wave of public indignation that a government official should participate in a gangster ceremony. One can only guess at the reams of patriotic prose and indignant denials to which we would be subjected in the United States if a similar situation were to be exposed.

Taoka accepted the badges of his office with solemnity and made a moving speech in which he asked his followers not to disgrace the name of the dead *oyabun*, and to follow him because of the example he would set rather than because they were obliged to. To himself he vowed that he would be an *oyabun* like Banzuiin Chobei, the first professional gambler to appear by name in Japanese crime history, around the middle of the seventeenth century, who had come down through history as a Robin Hood character, using his strength to uphold the weak against the powerful.

Taoka looked upon his entire life up to that point as a prelude: the early struggles, the profligate life, the murders, jail, violence, these were all behind him. Now he was seasoned and thoughtful, standing there among his *kobun* dressed in his white hemp suit and taking the oath of office. The real work was about to begin, the building of the Yamaguchi-gumi into the single most powerful underworld organization in Japanese history. Today Kobe, tomorrow Japan.

It was not simply growth for growth's sake he was after. As just another Kobe gang, he reasoned, the Yamaguchi-gumi would remain vulnerable. Any concerted police action could disband them, and because he was a realist, he knew such action would be inevita-

ble once the police regained their prewar strength. Nobody had ever accused the thirty-four-year-old Taoka
of cowardice, and though he was well aware of the odds
against this tiny nucleus of men defeating not simply
the forces of law and order, but the combined gangs
around the country, he was determined to take them all
on.

, Not in the usual, old-fashioned way, however. Swords
and guns would be only a last resort. He had come to
the same conclusion that Lucky Luciano had reached
some fifteen years earlier: that the surest way to success
was to ape the methods of big business. Corporate
holdings, that was the ticket. The Yamaguchi-gumi
would become a business organization with profitable
investments and legal-sounding "fronts" for their activities, which would furnish "employment" to all their
members. Bit by bit it would grow, swallowing up minor
competition along the way. One territory and then another, wherever there was a market for illegal activity,
there would be a Yamaguchi-gumi executive in charge
of running it. On that score, the police file on Taoka as
of now pays him the highest tribute for his unerring
judgment in picking and screening his henchmen.

And so began the reign of the third *oyabun* of the
Yamaguchi-gumi.

Ken Takakura as Taoka in the film *Yamaguchi-gumi.*

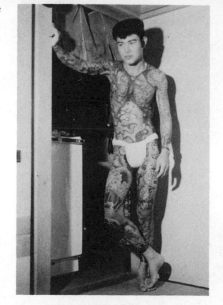

A yakuza.
(*Tadasu Izawa*)

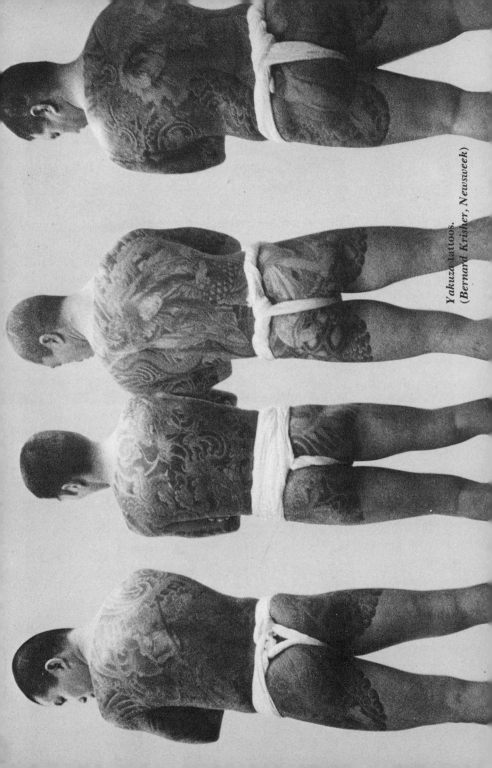

Yakuza tattoos.
(Bernard Krisher, Newsweek)

Kazuo Taoka, godfather of godfathers. (*S. Chang*)

A gang boss being led by members of his gang to a celebration in honor of his release from jail. (*Daily Yomiuri*)

Mitsuru Taoka, son of Kazuo Taoka.
(*S. Chang*)

CHAPTER 8

THE POLICE may well look back on those prewar times and the period immediately following the war as the good old days. At least the *yakuza* of those days stuck to the rules, their own rules to be sure, but rules. Their activities were well defined and their violence was directed against one another. Some gangs even had formal written charters containing certain strictures. One such, for instance, enjoined the membership not to do anything other than the regular "business," that is, gang business (gambling or prostitution in their own territory), even under the pressure of poverty. It also instructed them not to use ordinary language, but to practice the gang's special argot! In short, they wished to live in their own world and not to inflict themselves on the law-abiding society.

As of now, however, there is abroad in the land a new breed of gangster known as the *gurentai* who are blurring the boundaries and changing the picture, much to the consternation of the police and of the old-line *yakuza* as well. They do not even like to refer to this younger generation of gangsters as *yakuza*, which is a word with romantic images surrounding it. The word *gurentai*, on the other hand, stems from the verb *gureru*, "to turn bad," and *rentai*, "a military unit."

The *gurentai* have been on the scene since 1957, their entry having come when prostitution was outlawed and all the respectable brothel-keepers were put out of business. It had always been understood that street harlots, who were not legal, were the province of the *yakuza*. Every girl had her *himo* (which means "string") or *dani* (literally "parasitic worm"), both terms meaning "pimp," who was an accredited member of a gang, but the brothels were another matter. They were usually in the hands of perfectly decent pillars of the community, and there was no stigma attached to such ownership. Nor to patronizing them, for that matter, for the best people used the premises not only for the usual reasons, but often as places to entertain VIPs with tea ceremonies. When the brothels were closed by law, the *gurentai* moved in to keep them open. Violence was introduced where it had never existed, in precisely the same way as it had been in the United States when gangsters took over the liquor trade with the advent of prohibition.

Strong-arm men kept the prostitutes in line (they

were virtually prisoners in some cases, since many had wished to get out of the business in this new era), and the lower-class clientele which had replaced the cabinet ministers and industrialists as patrons were given to drunken brawling.

The *gurentai*'s toehold in the *yakuza* world started with prostitution, but they were not content to confine their activities to that, and soon they started their incursions into other businesses as well. The nightclubs, restaurants, bars and various branches of *mizushobai* where the old-line *yakuza* had been firmly entrenched as behind-the-scenes owners, silent partners, in charge of the personnel and hostesses who worked there, or as suppliers of food, drink and so on, found their power being challenged by the *gurentai*, who respected no tradition of territory and simply moved in with greater muscle. They did the same in the territory of established gambling games which had been run by *bakuto* groups, another designation for gangsters who used to specialize only in gambling. In less than two decades, the *gurentai* have so increased their power and have grown so prosperous that even the old-line *yakuza* who despise them can no longer ignore them, and most of the old-time gangs have been forced into alliances in which a *gurentai* mob acts as a subgroup to a big affiliation.

It would be foolhardy, to say nothing of very poor business, for the *yakuza* to refuse to have any truck with the *gurentai* on the grounds that they are not respecters of tradition. They take the long view that it is better to keep them as subsidiaries than to abdicate from the rich territories into which the *gurentai* have made such heavy inroads. Take Tokyo, for example; in any of the swinging districts such as the Ginza, Roppongi, Shinjuku, or Akasaka, you can't swing a cat in any direction without hitting a place to eat, drink and try to be merry at some of the most inflated prices in the world. Within the eight-block area which constitutes the Ginza, there are something like 1,150 bars and cabarets and about 400 restaurants, ranging in quality from haute cuisine to beanery. That's just the Ginza. The other districts are similarly wall-to-wall with places where high-livers spend lots of money, and while I should certainly not like to give the impression that every one of these places is "protected" or owned by *gurentai*, a considerable number of them are.

Where the *gurentai* have changed the picture of gangsterism in Japan is in their lack of reluctance to use violence on "honest citizens." Their methods of getting in on the action smack of the tactics of bully-boys which were perfected in the old Chicago days. A pair of *gurentai* hoods will approach the proprietor and advise him of a profit-sharing plan whereby they will "protect" the premises in return for a regular cut of the take. Protect them against themselves, that is to say. They will give him a little time to think things over, but should he demur, they drop by for something which gangsters refer to as *oreimairi*, which means literally "to say thanks," but which translates in their terms as busting up the place. Between beatings and vandalism, the proprietor usually gives in, unless he wants to close his business. If he's put his life savings into his work, chances are he'll go along. (I was quite impressed with the courage of my friend who owns a restaurant and who told me about his experience. "A couple of *gurentai* animals," he said, "came by one night and started

knocking pictures off the wall, breaking dishes and so
on. I watched them for a while, then I went over to
them, took their necks in my hands and beat their heads
together." My friend is a very tall and tough guy himself, but still . . . "And you scared them so that they
never came back?" I asked. "Well, that and the fact that
I called their *oyabun* who I happen to know and who
owed me a favor." Not everyone is that lucky.) But
that's the "protection" racket in certain kinds of businesses, and it adds up to quite a tidy sum, so while it
isn't actually old-line *yakuza* style, where they made
more formal deals and even contributed their share by
helping to attract patronage, they want to keep it in the
family and not let the *gurentai* put them out of business.

In addition to the clandestine houses of prostitution,
there are other places to look for girls if you're in the
market. The bars offer companions, as do the turkish
bathhouses, and other businesses which are in the
hands of *gurentai.* Of the turkish bathhouses in operation, approximately a quarter of them are in such
hands, and the police estimate that one in every three
turkish bath girls is a prostitute. Motels too, a fairly
recent phenomenon in Japan, are happy hunting
grounds, for the girls (although they have no actual
connection to the motels) are given to hanging around
in the bars and restaurants, and the rooms are right on
the premises. And some of these motels are also owned
outright by, are operated by, or have strong connections to *gurentai* mobs.

The *gurentai,* obviously sex specialists, have made an
excellent thing of porno, riding the crest of a rising
wave of sexual permissiveness. They raked in a hefty
eight hundred million yen in one year from the sale of

smuggled European and American girlie magazines, blue films and tapes with music and obscene dialogue. The police confiscated thousands of French postcards (with outlawed exposure, which in Japanese terms means the display of pubic hair), pornographic pictorials, reels of blue films in color, "obscene" cassette tapes, and other such material, and along the way they collared twenty-five hundred persons (including fifty foreigners, read Americans) involved in marketing these materials. Two-thirds of the people arrested were known members of *gurentai* gangs. Incidentally, what sold particularly well, if you're thinking of going into business, were the Scandinavian "nude magazines," especially the ones with pubic hair showing—that seems to turn the Japanese on—which alone accounted for one hundred million yen of the total.

The homemade products, blue films and obscene tapes, are made and distributed under the aegis of the *gurentai,* and they go much cheaper than the imported products which understandably call for a larger overhead expense. The smuggling, the payoffs, the contacts in other countries, these all cost money—and of course, there are the translations and dubbings which have to be made for their Japanese clientele. For these, a Tokyo *gurentai* mob hires students for the translations. It's a new wrinkle in working one's way through college.

All in all, sex is a good little business and the old-timers don't want to see it get out of their hands. Hence they hold their nose and make their deals with the *gurentai*—but not without misgivings and quite justifiable fears that they are the wave of the future.

Principally, what the traditional *yakuza* have against the *gurentai* is their life-style and their working habits,

which more closely resemble those of American mobsters than those of the *yakuza* of days gone by. Their
fear is that the random and unjustified violence against
non-*yakuza* of which they have been guilty will finally
succeed where the police have failed, in destroying the
romantic image which they have so carefully nurtured
of people who stick to their own world, an image which
has made large segments of the public regard them
tolerantly as "colorful." Even more important, the violence could force crackdowns which would send them
scurrying for cover. For the past three decades the
trend has been to buy into legitimate business, to present respectable fronts whenever possible, and to
represent themselves as honest citizens trying to earn
a living who are being harassed by police persecution.
And the police *have* been doing a lot of rounding-up.
In addition to those six thousand gangsters mentioned
earlier, it is not uncommon to see headlines which refer
to other thousands. Not enough to make a dent in the
total gangster population of one hundred fifty thousand, but a nuisance.

There is another point, a cultural difference—the
matter of the weapons which are preferred by the *gurentai:* they use guns. Taoka's weapon of choice was always
the sword. The iron-kettle incident was purely makeshift, nothing else having been available at the time, but
with him, as with other traditionalists, the sword is
more comfortable. I spoke with a mellow *yakuza,* a
grand sachem whom I met only as Mikki, and with
whom I went to a Kyoto restaurant in company with the
intermediary who introduced us. The restaurant was a
momma-poppa-run place, and they greeted Mikki with
affectionate deference, since, he told me, he had been

their original backer, and they politely tried to keep the puzzlement out of their faces at the strange trio we made—a Japanese businessman, a Japanese gangster, a middle-aged *gaijin*. The Japanese businessman speaks excellent English, and Mikki-san spoke some too—but even so, I had a hard time understanding the word *jingi* which kept coming into the conversation. Finally Mikki-san made it clear to me by saying, "When a man uses a gun, there is no *jingi*. *Gurentai* use guns because they do not understand *jingi*." *Jingi*, it seems, has to do with feelings of humanity, with a code of justice and of dignified respect which is involved even if your intention is murder.

"If I were to see a man pointing a gun at me," he said, "I would be afraid that yes, perhaps he would kill me, but it would not be the same kind of fear as if he were pointing a sword at me. A gun is cold. It is a machine. There is nothing personal about it. But a sword is a part of his own arm, of his own body, and I would feel his hatred as well as his sword going through my body." To my Western mind, getting killed is getting killed, but to my *yakuza* informant one kills or gets killed with honor or the whole act counts for nothing. He also taught me an expression which goes with running your sword through somebody's gut—"*Shinde moraimasu!*"—which means "I will have your life," or "Do me the honor of dying!" I have practiced it in non-*yakuza* circles, and it causes a stir, I can tell you.

Guns are showing up more and more in the police raids, along with the swords and knives which they confiscate, and stories of shoot-outs are also becoming commonplace. The guns are not easy to come by because of the tough, rigidly enforced gun-control laws, but a lucrative smuggling trade goes on just the same. The older *yakuza* may sit around and deplore the excesses of youth, but they are in somewhat the same position as the old dons of the mafia, to whom younger mafiosi contemptuously refer as "Mustache Petes." It's the generation gap all over again.

Bernie Krisher of *Newsweek* has told me that an *oyabun* he knows has talked to him at length about these newer, more violent gangsters. The *oyabun* is a man who is getting along in years, and would like to sit back and enjoy the fruits of his long and successful career. "If it were not for the *gurentai*," he says, "I would have retired long ago. I only stay active because I feel that restraining hands like my own are needed to keep them from committing acts which would bring massive storms of protest down upon our heads, and from the public as well as the police."

Krisher's *yakuza* friend is also disturbed, as are most other people, about another new wrinkle in the Japanese life fabric—the proliferation of adolescent gangs. The kids who belong to them are not to be compared to the adolescent Taoka, for example, who hung around the waterfront half starved and yearning for companionship, even the companionship of hooligans. These kids don't have the excuse of poverty or discrimination to account for their delinquency, nor are they interested in social causes or protest. In no way do they resemble the youth at the height of the violent days of the '60s in the United States, those who came out of middle- and upper-class suburbs and made common cause with the disadvantaged, or who were protesting the war in Vietnam. Nor are they city kids who have grown up in an atmosphere of turbulence and violence, of broken homes and rat-infested slums. These Japanese juvenile delinquents come from fair-to-middling families on the social and economic scale and they are called *chimpira,* a word which I was told stems from the Japanese word for "penis." I don't think the Japanese use the word "prick" as a term of opprobrium generally speaking, but that's certainly what they have in mind when they mention the *chimpira*—little pricks.

The well-behaved obedient Japanese youngster is such a stereotype in the minds of envious mothers in other parts of the world, including me, that I will admit to a moment of satisfaction when I learned that we weren't the only ones with problems. We've taken it on the chin from a lot of people for being overpermissive with our children, but nobody can accuse the Japanese of that, so "How come?" I started asking around. Herewith a mixed bag of answers:

Taoka: "The press and education system are ruining our children."

Reiko-san (a mother): "They pick up bad habits from going to American movies."

A sociologist: "The whole concept of adolescence is fairly new to Japan. We used to go straight into manhood from childhood, with the expectation of adult behavior from the moment of the cut-off. Now that we acknowledge in-between years we have in-between problems, and we look at them differently. What we used to regard as young *men* who were no good, we now see as juvenile delinquents, not yet men."

Historian: "Don't overlook the fact that Japan lost the war. The loss of authority in the older generation, the decline of their self-confidence affected our children profoundly. Your slum kids often grow up without a father and this has often been given as a reason for their delinquence. We had a whole generation of kids who grew up without a father in our terms—a strong figure who was the absolute authority. They started rejecting parental authority, since obviously it had proved not to be infallible. Once these kids started doubting the wisdom of their elders—not just their real parents, but all the parent symbols—things began to change. Some of them turned out to be the radical college youth who did all that rioting you saw on TV in the '60s, and some adopted the *yakuza* as their heroes and started behaving just like them. The process has gone on."

Whichever reason you buy, and there's probably validity in all of them, the fact remains that there are the *chimpira,* big as life, riding around on their motorcycles, scaring hell out of pedestrians and motorists, terrorizing their square schoolmates by practicing extortion and blackmail on them just like the grown-up *yakuza,* starting brouhahas at shrine festivals and generally making nuisances and worse of themselves.

The thing about them which is important is that they represent a new pool from which to recruit *yakuza* for adult gangs, and the signs are that they will follow the *gurentai* pattern of violence unrestricted by traditional behavior. They don't approach the savage proportions of America's own marauding street gangs which make taking an evening's stroll in most of our major cities an act of bravery, for they have not yet begun to bother the civilian population to any noticeable extent (although there have been some cases reported of assault by *chimpira*). Chiefly they confine their activities to their peers. But older *gurentai* keep an eye on them, and those who

are properly aggressive and ingenious can look forward
to an apprenticeship with a gang.

A few female adolescent gangs have sprung up too—
one of which consisted of ninety-odd girls from perfectly good, respectable families with satisfactory incomes. These little maids from school had important
matters to discuss over their sodas at the local sweet
shops: organizing assault, intimidation, blackmail and
shoplifting. And a little unorganized freelance whoring
as well. According to the police who broke up this ring,
the female delinquents are better organized and far
more vicious than the male, and they took special delight in beating up their schoolmates who were still
oriented to a kimono psychology of meek, submissive
female behavior. With so promising a crop, the *yakuza*
are certainly not going to suffer from a shortage of *suke*
to help them while away the time in the future.

CHAPTER 9

THE *YAKUZA* world in which Taoka started his reign as *oyabun* of the Yamaguchi-gumi was very different from the one which exists today. A modern *gurentai* would be more apt to choose Al Capone to model himself after than Banzuiin Chobei, whom Kazuo Taoka vowed to emulate.

Banzuiin had been a gambler, but he used gambling more as a come-on than as an actual occupation. Actually the games were his means of recruiting laborers, chiefly the good-for-nothing vagrants who roamed the countryside. It was the beginning of the seventeenth century—the Edo period (Edo being the original name of Tokyo)—and labor was needed to build the roads and to maintain the newly built castle. In other words, his activities were precisely those of the original Yamaguchi—serving as an agent to round up manpower, receiving commission from the men, and furnishing them with an opportunity to lose their pay by providing them with their favorite recreational pastime, gambling.

Banzuiin had a distinguished pedigree, what's more. He had been a samurai who had lost his master, hence his rank. Not his samurai arrogance, however, for even reduced as he was to the status of commoner, he and his *kobun* would dress themselves in elaborate kimonos and parade around Edo, calling themselves *machi-yakko*, which means "town guards," or "town samurai." They would look for other groups of racketeers of less elevated social standing, the *hatamoto-yakko*, who were merely the second or third sons of samurai families, and engage them in a spot of swordplay. The legend has made a Robin Hood of Banzuiin, robbing the rich to take care of the poor. The poor in Banzuiin's life were chiefly himself and his fellow gangsters, but that's a detail.

It might have been Banzuiin's habit of parading around town with his henchmen which gave Taoka his idea for making himself and the Yamaguchi-gumi household words. *He* knew who he was, and several mobs of Korean gangsters who were all too aware of his ability to wreak death and destruction knew who he was, but the Yamaguchi-gumi was not yet what could be called big-time, nor was Taoka a star to the general public.

He was determined to become one, and like Banzuiin, he made a regular routine of appearing in some public place with an older, tougher-looking senior member like Yoshikawa, plus an assortment of shills who would be scattered through the crowd. At a signal, the older member would reverently remove Taoka's shirt and start humbly washing his back, while the shills in the crowd would call everyone's attention to what was happening. There was always one to say, "Will you get a load of that squirt? Who does he think he is? Why should he rate all that attention?" Then someone else would reply, "Why that's Taoka, the famous *oyabun* of the Yamaguchi-gumi!" to be followed by "THAT'S Taoka? But he's so young!"

Even the hard-boiled police file is filled with admiration for the sheer gall of that play, and as an ex-advertising woman I applaud the direct approach. It's so simple-minded and effective—a bizarre device to tie in your three principal ingredients: Taoka, *oyabun*, Yamaguchi-gumi. You couldn't expect him to take an ad in the daily paper after all, so he had to work with what he had—to wit, gall. He got his message across pretty well: Taoka was the new boss of the Yamaguchi-gumi, he was smart and youngish, and watch your step, world. The police don't laugh at his tricks now and they didn't then either. In fact, they pay him tribute in their dossier by saying that his gift for publicizing himself and putting a good face on his deeds is unmatched in the history of Japanese gangs, even by Banzuiin Chobei.

The next order of business after establishing the brand name and the name of the boss was to go about making it seem like a legitimate organization by incorporating it as a construction company with himself as

managing director. Nothing got constructed, but the
members now received "salaries" instead of a share of
the take, and it was very nice to have a big wooden sign
over the entrance to their new headquarters which said
"Yamaguchi-gumi Construction Company."

Managing directors can't very well live like bums in
flats with their card-playing buddies, so Taoka moved
into a new house with Fumiko, now affectionately called
Anesan ("big sister") by the gang members, and with the
son for whom he had prayed—Mitsuru, who was then
three years old. There were also two servants and at all
times anywhere from eight to ten *kobun* who just hung
around, performing for him the same tasks which he
had performed for Big Eyes during his apprenticeship.
In addition, he records that the house was always filled
with young people, some of the wanderers left home-
less and hungry by the war. Taoka made sure that the
word got around that a bowl of rice was always available
at his home, and many of those who gathered to enjoy
his hospitality stayed on to join the Yamaguchi-gumi, as
they saw no future for themselves elsewhere in the
desolation of defeated Japan.

Taoka's feeling of responsibility toward these home-
less young men was genuine enough, but *giri* is a two-
way affair, and one assumes that certain services were
rendered in return. There was plenty of work for all
those employees of the Yamaguchi-gumi Construction
Company! Hands were needed to fight for territories,
to make collections from merchants and restaurateurs
who were "protected" by the Yamaguchi-gumi, hookers to be seen to, bars and cabarets and theaters to be
manned. Gang activities were still relatively unsophis-
ticated, concerned chiefly with the sporting life and the

illicit activities which surrounded it—smuggling drugs, gambling, harlotry, and the functions they performed in show business and labor recruitment. All these were chores which could be looked after by the *kobun* who enjoyed flexing their muscles and showing off for the boss. Taoka himself was occupied with working out a larger strategy for increasing the scope of their activities and for spreading the wings of the Yamaguchi-gumi out of Kobe and into other cities. The war had sent it all up for grabs by decimating the gangs who had controlled it, and Taoka saw no reason why his organization shouldn't do most of the grabbing.

The police weren't standing in his way as yet—it was other gang leaders who were just as determined to keep Taoka out of their territory as he was to get in. They would have to be dealt with one way or another before he could dominate the Kansai area. He wasn't even thinking of the Kanto area as yet—one thing at a time. Taoka worked out his strategy for expansion by concentrating his energies in the two areas he understood best —show business and the waterfront.

It was the late '40s, and there were still serious food crises and inflation. Taoka was deeply impressed by the fact that the more miserable the people were, the greater was their need for entertainment, to take their minds off their troubles. "Especially," he says, "movies and dance." As this was the case, he would provide them with entertainment. His first tentative move in that direction was to dig up a *rokyoku* singer named Haruhisa Kawada, whose popularity was slipping, but who seemed in Taoka's mind to have a very salable feature, the fact that he sang in a wheelchair as a result of tuberculosis of the spine. Taoka felt this was a psychological asset, for it matched the mood of the country which seemed also to be paralyzed, and if he could present this performer as singing bravely in the face of adversity, it would furnish inspiration to the audience. He played up this aspect for all it was worth in the publicity, and sure enough, he filled the newly built Shinkaichi Theater in Kobe night after night. Using this as a springboard, he got to the managers of other singers and let it be known that the Yamaguchi-gumi stood ready with financing and exploitation to help other artists. They were at first a little leery about getting themselves mixed up with gangsters, but times were tough and Taoka was persuasive, and before very long he had an impressive roster of performers under his aegis. In this way the Kobe Geinosha was born, a bona fide agency representing show business people through which the Yamaguchi-gumi functions in the entertainment world today.

It was not simply to help actors and to provide entertainment that Taoka wanted entry into that world. Take the *Home Run Hit Parade,* a show which Taoka put together starring his front runner, Hibari Misora (she of the gangster brother). The name of the show evoked two favorite Japanese preoccupations, baseball and pop singing, and was a great success. As such, it toured the country after it had opened in Osaka, and wherever it went, Yamaguchi-gumi men went with it to protect their property against incursions by local *yakuza.* Along the way, they also just happened to establish bases for themselves outside of Kobe, sometimes by making friendly affiliations with local gangs, sometimes by provoking incidents which resulted in wars in which they demonstrated superior strength. Even with such headliners as Misora, Izumi Yukimura, Michiya Mihashi and others of like stature under his wing, Taoka had no wish to become the William Morris Agency of Japan. He just wanted what looked like a legitimate front for other less legitimate activities, through which he could account for his income to the tax department and furnish jobs to his membership.

Now a reputation for violence isn't necessarily a bad thing to have in the gangster business. It could even be considered a business asset, and the Yamaguchi-gumi did its best to foster that reputation, even in their show business activities. Naturally the dignified *oyabun* took no personal part in instances involving bloodshed, but he couldn't very well help it if now and again things happened where arms had to be taken up to save somebody's face—especially his.

For instance, there was the incident involving Koji Tsuruta, who is one of the country's leading stars in *yakuza* movies. The Tsuruta incident occurred around 1950, by which time Taoka and the Yamaguchi-gumi were firmly established in the world of entertainment, and Taoka had had occasion to perform a service for Tsuruta, for which he was very grateful. He was so grateful that he sent his manager around to call on Taoka with a message of thanks. The manager presented Taoka with a gift of seaweed, a traditional gift which he accepted graciously. Unfortunately the manager also tried to give him a gift of cold, hard cash, which Taoka in his dignity considered to be an insult, and which he pushed back in the manager's face. You don't offer to tip the *oyabun* and Taoka sent him packing with several harsh words. That, however, was not the end of it. Taoka's *kobun*, upon hearing of the insult to their *oyabun*, rushed over to the hotel where Tsuruta was staying, broke into his room, assaulted him with a whisky bottle, slashing him on the head and hands. Tsuruta fell to his knees, begged for his life and worded an apology to be conveyed to the *oyabun*. The attack ended and they left him bleeding copiously from many wounds.

Tsuruta managed to get himself to a hospital, where they stitched him up, but because he was quite famous, word of the assault got around and the police started rounding up Yamaguchi-gumi members for questioning. Nothing came of it for Taoka, but the incident is noteworthy because it marked the only recorded case of defection in the ranks of the Yamaguchi-gumi. One of the *kobun* told the police that it was Taoka who had ordered the attack. Nobody knows what became of him, or of Tsuruta's manager for that manner, but the apology had evidently been sufficiently humble, for Taoka now speaks of Tsuruta as a friend.

During this period, the late '40s and early '50s, another powerful criminal syndicate, called the Honda-kai, was elbowing the Yamaguchi-gumi for domination of the Kansai area. Honda, not to be confused with the fellow who makes motorcycles, was a very different personality from Taoka and the two *oyabun* attracted different types among their followers. Those who ran to Taoka's side were attracted to his reputation for violence and to the excitement and glamor of show business. They took great pleasure in their growing reputation as crazy hooligans who would stop at nothing, while those who rallied around Honda were chiefly *bakuto*, traditional gamblers, more conservative in their approach and more sensitive to the order of society. Honda himself held the view that problems could be solved by discussion, and he had already established a firm base in the construction business in Kobe by the time he formed the Honda-kai to amalgamate the gamblers' groups under one parent organization. His business-man's personality was more attractive to those *yakuza* groups who were afraid of the violence of the Yamagu-chi-gumi, and there were enough of them to put the Honda-kai on an equal footing with the Yamaguchi-gumi for sheer numbers. Neither Honda nor Taoka had anything against each other personally, nor did Taoka feel ready for a head-on collision with so powerful a group. He and Honda had in fact shared a brotherhood cup on a fifty-fifty basis to demonstrate their mutual respect, and for many years they maintained the bal-ance of terror between them.

However, just as with corporations which keep get-ting to be bigger and bigger conglomerates, it's hard for the executives to keep their finger on the pulse of all their affiliate members, and the amity between Honda and Taoka did not necessarily extend to affili-ates in other towns. Honda found his power being eroded by some dissident members who envied the success of the more violent Yamaguchi-gumi tactics and began some internal skullduggery to unseat their *oya-bun*. They wanted a more aggressive *oyabun,* and a rift developed in the ranks between those who wanted to hang on to Honda and those who were pressing for a dangerous hothead named Hirata. He was agitating for an all-out gang war against the Yamaguchi-gumi to make the Honda-kai the most powerful organization in the Kansai area. Still under the Honda-kai umbrella, Hirata formed a group which he called the Asia Youth

Peace Maintenance Army, which combined gangster and rightist activities. He picked up twenty-four branches in and out of Kobe, making it the largest of the Honda-kai line.

One of these affiliates was situated in the town of Komatsujima, on the island of Shikoku where Taoka had been born. The Yamaguchi-gumi had an active mob there too, for Komatsujima is a harbor town, and as such there is quite a flourishing amusement area, with cafes, *pachinko* parlors, juke-box joints and various other attractions for the merchant seamen who fill the streets looking for action. This was lucrative territory for the gangster mobs who dominated them. There had been occasional skirmishes between the hostile factions, but none serious enough to bring the parent organizations into the battle.

Taoka's memoirs describe a different sort of skirmish which started in the upstairs office of a *pachinko* parlor on a bright festival day. The streets were filled with pleasure-seekers, men dressed in holiday kimonos with the divided skirts drawn up between their legs and tucked into their sashes, and the women were wearing their holiday kimonos too, mincing around in their *geta* (Japanese wooden clogs). There was dancing in the street, and the laughing, shouting crowd filled every pleasure spot along the way. The *pachinko* parlor was filled to overflowing, and the deafening clangor of the steel *pachinko* balls plus loud juke-box music mixed with the din of voices. Hardly anyone noticed the little group of men edging their way carefully through the crowd toward the staircase leading to the office. They were dressed like everybody else, and nobody was looking for the outline of their swords under their kimonos, or was paying any attention to the leader who was holding his hands to his breast to cover the gun he was carrying.

They were members of a Yamaguchi-gumi affiliate, and as they broke into the office they unsheathed their weapons and faced the Honda-kai affiliate members: "You've gotten a little too hungry for your own good," they told them. "You're just a lousy bunch of *tekiya* and you've been branching out into gambling. We own the gambling in this town. What have you got to say?" The Honda-kai group members had nothing to say. They just looked at each other and drew their swords. Within minutes one man lay dead and four others seriously wounded, and the tiny upstairs office was a sea of blood.

It was the opening incident in a series of battles which became more and more complex, drawing in other groups which were all related to one or the other parent body, the Yamaguchi-gumi or the Honda-kai. The original incident was all but forgotten and the Yamaguchi-gumi affiliate may well have rued the day they started it all, since the Honda-kai people were more powerful in the area, with many more groups and men at their disposal. However, the local *oyabun* of the Yamaguchi-gumi group was an important fellow, a man who had started his career as a longshoreman, had later engaged in marine transportation business, and by one of those curious circumstances which amazed me each time I heard of them, he had been elected as an assemblyman in the city. An American politician, an important one as it happens, told me I was naive if I supposed that the mafia hasn't elected members to jobs in big-city machines. I suppose they have, but at least it's not so open and would be, I'm sure, vehemently denied. In any case, this *oyabun* had had a brotherhood relationship with

Noboru Yamaguchi through his involvement with long-shoremen, and as such he felt absolutely justified in calling upon his successor, Taoka, for assistance. His continued existence as a gang leader depended on poppa coming through for him.

Poppa didn't especially want to, nor did the executives of the Honda-kai look forward to a confrontation with Taoka's men, so they met in joint session to try to iron out a cease-fire with enough face-saving devices to satisfy both factions. The word went back to Komatsujima and both sides seemed to agree, but a piece of treachery on the part of the Honda-kai made it flare up again: a Yamaguchi-gumi man was ambushed and shot through the back, the thigh and the belly. The Komatsujima police knew they were in for a rough time, and they picked up a few of the Honda-kai men and placed a cordon around the city.

Back at Kobe headquarters, the Yamaguchi-gumi was stunned by this turn of events and Taoka decided he had had enough of tiptoeing with the Honda-kai. He went about the business of mobilizing his men, sending out juniors to round up every member who could be found, at their hangouts, their offices, their homes, their mistresses' homes. They were to get stirring, go to Komatsujima by the next boat and settle the matter. As Michio Sasaki, now *oyabun* of the Sasaki-gumi recalls it: "I was watching some sumo wrestlers when this *kobun* came to me with the news. I could hardly believe it, for I thought the matter was to be settled without any war. I was instructed to set out for Komatsujima that very day, and naturally I did." As did a few hundred other good men and true.

As the Kobe police had been alerted to the situation,

they gathered at Kobe port to try to persuade the gang members not to go. They could hardly prevent them, as they searched their luggage and found no arms, but they could try to talk them out of it.

"How can you ask us," the Yamaguchi-gumi men replied, "to stay away from visiting our brother who is in the hospital and who has been shot?"

"So many of you?" the police asked.

"Many more wished to go," the Yamaguchi-gumi men replied. "They all have *giri* toward our brother."

"In that case," the police said, "we'll just go along to help *our* brothers, the Komatsujima police." Which they did.

It was this speedy mobilization more than the actual fighting which proved to be the most demoralizing to the Honda-kai affiliate. Hundreds of enemy gangsters plus some four hundred assembled police arriving within hours seemed to point up to them that the Honda-kai was outclassed when it came to aggressive action, and the rift which had been fostered by Hirata began to deepen. They gestured that they would surrender, and they sent an emissary to police headquarters to meet with a Yamaguchi-gumi representative to effect peace. The Yamaguchi-gumi agreed to pull their men out of Komatsujima, except for a cadre of vigorous enforcers in case trouble started up again. But the lesson had come across loud and clear, and the power of the Honda-kai was on the wane as of that day, with affiliates deserting to join with their former enemies. A rather dazzling piece of psychological warfare which was not lost on the rest of the *yakuza* world throughout the country.

Each successful battle, whether bloody or strategic,

brought new groups flocking to the Yamaguchi-gumi. The Meiyu-kai war which had started with the "Blue Castle Incident" ended with the Yamaguchi-gumi in absolute control of Osaka through their affiliates. One of these affiliates is worthy of mention as it is the only Korean group which is a part of the Yamaguchi-gumi. It is called the Yanagigawa-gumi, and is led by a man named Jiro Yanagigawa, a name which he has adopted because it sounds more Japanese than his own name, Yang. He had founded something called the Yanagigawa Development Company, which then became the Yanagigawa-gumi, and his action captains had names like Kang, Dong Wha and So Moo Won. It interested me that Taoka does not allow his racism to interfere with his business acumen. Yanagigawa is obviously better within the ranks than he would be as an enemy, a very smart fellow himself who manages a construction company, a promotion company, a sports sheet called the *Osaka Hochi Newspaper*, and has enough financial backing through his various enterprises to enable him to knock out *yakuza* competition whenever it turns up. He has extended his influence from Osaka to Hyogo, Nara, Wakayama, Kyoto, Shiga and the entire Kinki district. He has also successfully fought his way into Gifu, Mie and Aichi prefectures, and his seemingly endless expansion has continued to Fukui, Ishikawa, Toyama, Nigata in the Hokuriku district and up as far as Hokkaido. Korean or not, he is certainly an indispensable member of the inner council of the Yamaguchi-gumi, where he has sat since he exchanged his brotherhood cup in the '50s.

He is not only very smart, he is very tough. Nobody tries to invade his territories with impunity. One who did try had in mind opening a *pachinko* parlor in a district where Yanagigawa held sway. The man was warned in person to stay out of town, but he foolishly persisted in coming. He never arrived, because on the train two fellow travelers approached his seat, addressed him by name, and when he stood to respond, they stabbed him in each side. They then waited for the train to slow down for a curve and jumped out of the window amid the horrified screams of the passengers who had witnessed the event. With allies like Yanagigawa, Taoka need never concern himself with details.

There have been times too when taking over a territory has happened fortuitously, totally unplanned. For example, there was a man around Osaka a few years back named Ginji Yosakura, who was an enforcer for the Yamaguchi-gumi. Ginji had participated in the "Blue Castle Incident" with the Meiyu-kai, and he was hiding out from the police.

Now Ginji was one of those strange phenomena who turn up now and again in *yakuza* movies, a rebel who makes trouble for his brothers and usually winds up very dead. He was, in fact, so much of an oddball that a book has been written about him in which he is described as a smart and beautiful killer, but his associates do not hold him in such high esteem. An old-time member of the Yamaguchi-gumi was quoted as saying, "Ginji was called the number one marksman for the Yamaguchi-gumi, but there were many better ones. He wasn't that talented." Maybe that was just professional jealousy, but more likely the dislike of his brother gangsters stems from the fact that Ginji was that most despised breed among *yakuza*—a man who preferred to operate as a lone wolf.

His eccentricities got on everyone's nerves. He kept his distance from group members and seniors, and he always carried big bankrolls with him—the equivalent of a thousand dollars at a time—because for one thing, he was addicted to gambling, at which he hadn't much skill. Generally he lost, and when he did he would fly into a rage, scream that he had been cheated, and raise his gun in the air demanding his money back. When he was turned down he would fire the gun and create a riot. As the critic quoted above on the subject of his marksmanship put it, "His behavior wasn't good," which should win some kind of award for understatement.

When things got too hot for him in Osaka, Ginji took off for a town called Fukuoka, which is located in the center of a big mining area. There he knew there was a Yamaguchi-gumi affiliate called the Iishii-gumi, but there were other *yakuza* groups who were more important. Ginji presented himself to the *oyabun*, Ichiro Iishii, submitted his credentials, called upon the "family" to help him if he should need it, and was accepted as an out-of-town relative in good *yakuza* tradition.

He chose Fukuoka for the very good reason that he had a rich financial source to draw upon there, a mine owner who had once used Ginji's services as a hit man in a labor problem when some left-wingers had tried to form a union. Ginji had been paid very well, about twenty thousand dollars, but unfortunately for the mine owner, Ginji's newly developed taste for cash had him showing up time and again for further payment, anywhere from five hundred dollars to one thousand dollars at a clip. He needed every cent of it to pay for some expensive habits he had acquired—women, alcohol and gambling.

Ginji was a nocturnal animal, hiding in his apartment by day, stalking the neon-lit section by night dressed like an American gangster out of a '30s film, tightly belted raincoat, upturned collar and black slouch hat pulled down low on his forehead. He went from bar to bar, rarely speaking to anyone except to order his drinks, smoking foreign cigarettes and ignoring the light offered by bar girls, which made him seem intriguing and mysterious. That, together with the fact that he was a prodigious tipper, throwing the equivalent of twenty-five dollars on the bar, succeeded in attracting quite a coterie of hostesses who would show up at his apartment two at a time to sample his virility. There he would greet them in kimono, and they were excited and stimulated by his violence of manner, by the tattooing on his back and by the fact that even when he made love to them, his trusty Colt revolver was right under his pillow.

His gambling skill had not improved since his Osaka days, and he found himself in trouble in a game run by a rival mob, the Miyamoto-gumi, where he not only fired his pistol but had the bad judgment to take a swing at the *oyabun* himself, Miyamoto. He made his escape, but naturally his life was on the line from that moment, and he made himself scarce at the bars which he had frequented, and put a moratorium on hostesses, even going so far as to send for his wife to come and stay in the apartment.

He woke up one cold January morning in 1962 with a fever and chills. He was due at a party that night for a friend who had just come out of jail, but when the time arrived to leave for the party, he felt so weak that he told his wife to go along without him, and to send for a masseur before she left. Since the Miyamoto incident he had been extremely careful to keep his door bolted at all times, but in his weakened condition and expecting a masseur, he overlooked the precaution this one time—a fatal mistake. Two men entered silently, four shots sounded and Ginji lay dead on his tatami mat, shot through the throat, chest and abdomen, his trusty Colt still under his pillow, safety catch in place.

His brother *yakuza* Ichiro Iishii wept at the news of his death, deploring the fact that Ginji had not had a chance to defend himself, and the Yamaguchi-gumi was called upon to avenge him. Love for their reckless black-sheep brother did not motivate them so much as the opportunity to take over still another territory, for the Miyamoto-gumi was an affiliate of a powerful gang who dominated the district, called the Oshima family. The senior executives of the Yamaguchi-gumi went into session and the decision was made: "Let's go to Ginji's funeral."

The word was passed around, and the black-clad Yamaguchi-gumi men began boarding the train at Kobe. As it stopped at various stations along the way to its destination, other men in black boarded and by the time the train arrived at Fukuoka there were a hundred gang members aboard. Later trains brought more hundreds, and the police began to prepare for action, spreading cordons and patrols around the hotels and houses where the gang members were staying. When they were questioned, they responded again with the excuse of *giri* as they had when they visited their sick friend in the hospital at Komatsujima. This time, however, the police search turned up an assortment of pistols, carbines, rifles, long swords and short swords—quite an arsenal for a funeral—and the police arrested a total of one hundred five men. The action was temporarily halted, but after the initial alert had died down a new arsenal found its way into town, and the war was on. It continued for several weeks with the usual results—the territory fell to the Yamaguchi-gumi. Ginji Yosakura, a nuisance to his brothers in life, had done them a service with his death.

But the story has a kicker. It was not the Miyamoto-gumi which had been responsible for Ginji's death. It was the mine owner who had had it with Ginji's continuing demands and had sent around the hit men to dispose of the problem permanently.

While all these incidents were serving to consolidate the power of the Yamaguchi-gumi in the Kansai area, Taoka was also working out his plan to dominate the rich waterfront territory. He had dissolved his first corporate venture, the Yamaguchi-gumi Construction Company, and founded another, the Longshoremen's Development Company, whose purpose, as he describes it, was "to improve and promote the living standard and unity of longshoremen." He invited other *oyabun* to join him in this venture, heads of "families" not actually allied to him, but not unfriendly. He asked company heads in Yokohama, and as a means of getting his feet wet in political circles, he courted the Minister of Construction, Ichiro Kohno, and asked him to sit on the board of directors, which he agreed to do. Much of his financing came from a right-wing extremist, an ex-member of the Japanese Communist Party by the name of Seigen Tanaka (no relation to the Prime Minister) who had seen the light of the right and who felt Taoka was a fellow well worth cultivating to fight the left-wing influences among dock workers.

Taoka was returning to the waterfront as though to a first love. Noboru Yamaguchi, during his tenure as *oyabun,* had rather neglected the harbors in favor of show business, but Taoka had an affection for this atmosphere where he had known the first warmth of human relationship in his life. And he felt a kinship with the outcasts who wrested their wretched livelihoods out of the harbors and who lived in the *gonzo-heya,* the prisonlike barracks which lined both sides of the streets from the Public Employment Security Office to the waterfront. Reeking of sweat and cheap whisky, these *gonzo-heya* were packed with human derelicts. Those who could not scrape up the amount of yen for even such miserable accommodations slept in the street. In describing them to me, the socialist friend who had refused to let me go and see them said, "Just to say they stink would be like saying the Black Hole of Calcutta was uncomfortable."

During the occupation, the United States military authority had issued orders to "democratize" the harbor, but the Ministry of Labor was still somewhat lacking in experience in what that meant, and the voice of a lot of miserable, underpaid and underfed laborers carried no weight. The U.S. orders had been that only major warehouses were to handle the freighting contracts, but there was no way they could control the reletting of those contracts to subcontractors and sub-subcontractors, most of whom were *yakuza.* Between the original contractors down the line to the subs and sub-subs, around sixty percent of the commissions were raked off, which left very little to pay the low men on the totem pole—the workers who did the backbreaking work on the docks.

Taoka may have been moved by some sentimentality to enter the picture, but there were other, rather more practical reasons. As he has said, "Japan is surrounded by sea. It is very evident that Japan has to depend widely on the harbors for trade." The development of the harbors was necessary for the reconstruction of Japan, and the money that could be made from controlling those harbors was necessary to the reconstruction of the Yamaguchi-gumi. At the time that Taoka entered the harbor picture, it was not just Japan but the United States which was depending on those harbors, for the Korean War had broken out and every available man was needed to work the docks through which supplies for the U.S. Army were carried.

There were not enough registered workers to fill this need, and Taoka was approached by the big warehouse companies to use his old talents for recruiting unregistered workers. Although this was not in line with U.S. policy, the warehouse owners felt that GHQ would be none the wiser, and besides they seemed to have no real understanding of the problem. The registered workers had begun organizing labor unions and were making noises about wage increases. To fight them openly would give them bad marks with the U.S. authority, but Taoka, they felt, knew how to go about these things, and the men he would recruit would be more tractable. Of course, they had no idea that Taoka himself would start leaning on them for a better break for the men who carried his standard. He planned to have absolute control of the waterfront, and he understood perfectly that to get a lot, you give a little.

He was an old hand at winning loyalty and confidence from his men, and he demonstrated it when a ship loaded with unsealed sulfur arrived from the United States. The contract to unload it was brought to Taoka, who knew that the fumes of the sulfur, which would be absorbed into the pores of the sweating men, were poisonous, would cause dizziness and sometimes worse, and that there were bound to be casualties from the inhalation of these poisons. He wanted the contract badly, but he felt the company should pay something extra for the risks that were involved.

They turned him down. "Your job," they said, "is to load and unload, not to make policy. If you don't want the job there are plenty of others who do." That was certainly true, and a grandstand play seemed called for.

"Okay," he said, "but I'll make you a sporting proposition. I'm going to work on this personally, and I invite you to join me just to see what it's like. Then we'll see what you have to say."

They did not wish to appear cowardly, so a few company officials joined him at the docks and they started unloading under the glaring sun. It took less than half an hour for them to yell "uncle," after one of their number had fainted from the fumes and the others were looking green around the gills. They gave Taoka what he wanted.

News spreads quickly along the waterfront, and before long the waterfront workers recognized in Taoka one of their own and flocked to his ranks. He actually did get them more money, he actually did fight for better living conditions for them, and eventually he unified them into something he regarded as a proper labor union, which he called the Kobe Harbor Labor Union.

He managed also to elbow out his *yakuza* competition who were engaged in the same kind of subcontracting as he was, and there were many bloody battles fought, although he virtuously denies that the Yamaguchi-gumi was doing anything wrong. "Everybody always accuses us of violence," he virtuously states in his memoirs, "but we did not have to commit violence. We simply knew better how to do our job. The people who were doing these bad things, when they got caught, would use our name and put the blame on us."

As his business grew he established something called the Koyo Forwarding Company Ltd., and encouraged some of the more talented among his *kobun* to start their own forwarding companies too. Three of them— Aoi, Katani and Yasuhara—followed his advice, and among the four of them they managed to lock up most of the harbor business in fairly short order.

Taoka's waterfront labor organization was regarded contemptuously by other unions as being a tool of the companies. This made him quite angry, for he doesn't like being referred to as a capitalist or as a tool of capitalists. "They accuse me of having a kept union," he has said, "but you don't have to carry a red flag to be on the side of the worker. What's the use of strikes and picketing and tearing the company apart? If there's no company there's no work." This view is somewhat reminiscent of what some of our more rugged individualists regard as the halcyon days, the era of Big Daddyism when labor unions were relatively powerless. However, to enforce his protestations of genuine concern for the working stiffs, Taoka was able to produce a testimonial from Genichi Sujita, who was at that time the head of the Longshoremen Public Employment Agency: "When Mr. Taoka started showing up at the harbor there was great disorder and violence. The life of a longshoreman was unbearable—much worse than a beggar's life. Mr. Taoka approached the Ministry of Labor again and again to improve the situation, and thanks to him the first dormitory for longshoremen was built. He also labored for the establishment of a workmen's hospital in Kobe. If Mr. Taoka weren't in the *yakuza* world, he would surely be a great asset to the political field."

Dragging out the red herring is always a workable device, and Taoka is very skilled at it. He may even believe in himself as a defender against a communist takeover, but his fears as of now hardly seem justified where the labor movement is concerned. Which is not to say that there is not a militant left wing, but even my socialist friend was not too sanguine about their chances for gaining power. I saw him several times after that initial lunch at the Imperial Hotel, and it was over cocktails at the Press Club to which I had invited him that he told me, "Every time genuine militant working-class people try to start a real union where it is needed, like at the mines or on the waterfront, *yakuza* are called in. There have been many murders."

Actually it is not simply *yakuza* activity which prevents the formation of a working-class movement of any great strength, but the splinter groups within the ranks of labor itself and the divisions of political thought, which include conservatives, right-wing socialists, and middle-of-the-road socialists whose views resemble British

Fabianism rather than Marxism. It would take a genuine economic disaster for the factions of the labor movement to forget their internal differences and become unified.

In fact, it seemed to me that worker solidarity runs a poor second to company loyalty among workers. We have our share of eager beavers in the United States, but our general attitude about jobs is that the companies for which we work are entitled to our devotion from nine a.m. to five p.m., after which we are free to go home and burn wax effigies of the boss if that's our idea of fun. According to Japanese sociologist Chie Nakane, this is by no means true of the Japanese worker. His loyalty works around the clock, and his devotion to *oyabun* and company matches that of the *yakuza kobun* to his *oyabun* and criminal organization. The *oyabun*, it must be stressed, may have achieved his place through seniority, but he keeps it through consensus. His principal attribute is his capacity to maintain harmony. Both *oyabun* and *kobun*, legitimate or otherwise, learned their roles from the traditions of their society, which places such stress on filial obedience and respect for authority. The employee's union is a company union (bane of existence to our AFL-CIO boys); his friends are company friends; his recreation, often his housing, social life and health programs, are provided for by the company. A machinist who works for company A makes no identification with machinists who work for company B. His fortunes lie with his company, and the more prosperous that company, the better he sees his life as being. In addition, lifelong employment has been a traditional factor in Japanese industry, so there you are. He lives in a web of tradition, but the tradition all around him is changing slowly and increasing freedom in all aspects of life could affect the values and practices of the working man. With that in mind, management keeps a wary eye open, constantly emphasizing through company activities and literature the mutual interests of company and worker, and those in the fold who think differently are regarded as pariahs by boss and fellow employees alike, who genuinely feel that the prosperity of the organization redounds to all of their benefit, that their mutual welfare is threatened by divisive action.

Independent unions are not likely to start up in any of the great corporations of Japan, but in case they do, the *yakuza* are always available to break them up. Just call your friendly neighborhood *oyabun* to whom you may have given the title of "Business Consultant, Labor Relations Expert," and he'll be glad to be of service. Makes you a little nostalgic, doesn't it? *O tempore! O mores!* O Henry Ford and your "security police" which strove so valiantly to keep the United Auto Workers from invading your domain!

There is small danger that Taoka's waterfront organization, the Koyo Forwarding Agency, or his other front, the Kobe Geinosha, which takes care of his show business activities, stands in much danger of being taken over by communists. Nor is it simple naiveté which makes him rail against them. It is the time-honored sure-fire ploy of the man who has something to hide which raises the specter of communism to divert attention from his deeds.

CHAPTER 10

CONSIDERING the estimated annual income of the Yamaguchi-gumi, Taoka has been doing something right. If I had known, when I spoke with Mitsuru Taoka, about those billions of yen which fall into the pocket of the Yamaguchi-gumi, I'd have made him a counteroffer: instead of ten percent of my royalties, I'd settle for ten percent of their annual take-home pay, to quietly pack my bags and go home.

To find out where those billions came from, I asked Mr. Chang if he could arrange for me to meet with the police. He called his contact, Mr. Nakahira, Chief of the Second Section of the National Police Agency, which is the section that concentrates on and coordinates *yakuza* activity throughout the country, then called me back and said, "It's in the works. I'll get back to you."

He did. Three or four times, in fact, over a period of a few weeks, during which time I never went out of my hotel room without leaving exact messages as to where I could be reached—or if that was impossible, I kept phoning in to make certain I hadn't missed the summons. It certainly was no fault of Mr. Chang that setting up such a meeting was almost as difficult as setting up the one with Taoka-san. Even he had not expected this to be so, and he was almost as puzzled as I was. First Mr. Nakahira had said yes, he would see me, then no, then yes again and then no, etc. I had almost given up on the idea and concluded that I had probably come at a bad time of the year, for the "no" was always on a perfectly valid basis. The Diet was in session and the department was on constant alert; Mr. Nakahira had been called into an important conference; he had had to leave town on urgent and unexpected business. Mine not to reason why, mine but to wait for Mr. Chang to call and tell me to come running before Mr. Nakahira could change his mind again.

Mr. Chang disagrees with me, but I think the genuine reason for the postponements emerged when Mr. Nakahira finally was worn down by Mr. Chang's insistence and said I could come, and then added, "Why does this *gaijin* (foreigner) wish to expose our national shame?" Mr. Chang, in relating this to me, had no idea that I would seize upon it as a uniquely Japanese attitude. For me, it contained one of the answers to the question which had brought me so far; it had sent me into improbable rendezvous with a gangster at a *sushi* bar, with the godfather in Kobe, with an *oyabun* in Kyoto, with businessmen and sociologists and psychoanalysts and socialists, with journalists to jails—all places where I suppose I must have seemed very much out of context. The question had been "How could a criminal underground of such vast proportion be kept practically a secret from the rest of the world?" And now look where Tokiko-san's slit throat had led me—to police headquarters in Tokyo.

Mr. Nakahira's reference to national shame becomes more understandable if you look at the map. It will show you that Japan is not quite as large as the state of California. Within that space there is a population of almost one hundred nine million, according to the latest census figures, and that population is almost perfectly homogeneous. To this foreigner it sometimes felt as though it were one enormous family living under one roof, all deeply connected to one another by reasons of tradition, history, code of ethics, language, upbringing. We, on the other hand, are a nation of foreigners—some of us more recent than others—and we're given to referring to "them" when we speak of groups of different ethnic backgrounds from the one to which we belong. The mafia, we say, is something that comes from Sicily. It's foreign. It's "them." Never mind that it's been around for enough generations to make them as American as the rest of us. It's still "them."

In Japan they speak of "us," the only exception being those Oriental minorities who live in their midst, the Koreans and Chinese, and even they are racial brothers, usually indistinguishable to foreigners from the Japanese. The "us" they speak of includes their gangsters, and Mr. Nakahira is deeply ashamed of these black sheep who are putting a blot on the family escutcheon. It seemed to me that he sees himself not just as a cop with a job to do, but as a family member trying to clear the family name. Every Japanese with whom I ever spoke is sensitively aware of the impression his country makes on the rest of the world. It goes beyond patriotism. It is, as I said, a family affair.

As they are such a homogeneous people, it follows that their gangsters who have been exposed to all the same traditions, history and so forth, should faithfully copy the only society they know about in building their underground society. Even though it is a grotesque caricature, one can find a precedent in the establishment for most of their customs and their social behavior, so it's hard for a foreigner to tell the players without a score card.

Take a small example, like the common practice in Japan of exchanging name cards. I have collected a shoe-box full of cards, and have added to it every time I was introduced to a new person. This is not simply a bit of *politesse*—it is an exchange of dossiers which are supposed to help you determine your behavior toward the man who gave it to you. Most cards not only give you a name, they give you the name of the company for whom the person works and the position held in that company (unless he is so famous that he doesn't need all that information on his card). It also contains any other credits he thinks worth noting. An author I know who doesn't work for a company had engraved on his card a list of the books he had written and the countries in which he had lectured, for example. In any case, if your new acquaintance lists credits which are better than your own, you bow a little lower than he does and vice versa, and you also know what honorific form to use in addressing him. He may be *sensei*, which is teacher, or master, or something very respectful, or just plain *san*, which is Mr., Mrs., or Miss. (Not Ms. It is a possibility for the future, but not quite yet.) Now it just so happens that in my shoe-box of cards I have a number which came from gangsters. One of them, from a beautifully polite young man, says that he is a member of the Sasaki-gumi (which as I have said is an affiliate of the Yamaguchi-gumi) and that he is a captain of a youth group in the gang. The gang insignia is engraved on the card as well. Well now, can you imagine a mafioso getting cards engraved saying, "Gambino family soldier. Specialty: enforcer"?

Even the "family" setup of the *yakuza* which had seemed to me in my ignorance to be modeled after the mafia is actually a copy of the rest of society, the "vertical structure" which Chie Nakane speaks of in her book. The strong figure at the top who speaks for the entire clan, the loyal and obedient members, as Jiro Tamiya had told me early on—that's how it works in every aspect of the society, in the home, in business, in school, everywhere—and it is ingrained in every Japanese from birth, whether he grows up to manufacture steel or to steal from manufacturers. "That," Bernard Krisher told me, "is why a movie like *The Godfather* was such a smash here. Sure, it was exciting on its own, and the Japanese are big fans of gangster films generally, but this one had a special meaning which they could relate to because of the family relationship. It closely parallels a Japanese family where everyone has his designated place in a set hierarchy." In this non-Christian-Judaeo society, it would appear that "Honor thy father" is *really* a commandment. In middle Japan, mother rules the roost in actuality, but father is the spokesman. Albeit there has been some erosion of authority among certain segments of the society, on the whole, you still don't find many Japanese kids telling their fathers they don't know where it's at.

You can get pretty paranoid hanging around and waiting for a phone to ring, and I knew in my bones when I woke up that August morning and heard on my radio that it was expected to be the hottest day of the year, that this would be the day Mr. Nakahira would clear time to see me. Never mind that it was just as hot for him as it was for me. Never mind that he was doing me a favor, one which he had indicated he wasn't wildly happy about doing. The will-he-won't-he-see-me routine had gotten under my skin and I had reached the point, in fact, where I wished he would tell me to get lost and have done with it. I mention all this to explain why, when the phone rang and Mr. Chang said, "Can you be downstairs in ten minutes? Mr. Nakahira is free this afternoon," it was almost an anticlimax and I muttered "Okay" rather than "Oh, marvelous!" which he had every right to expect.

My mood didn't improve as I moved through the revolving door from the refrigerated lobby of the Imperial into the oven of Tokyo, and when I climbed into the cab in which Mr. Chang drew up, I didn't think to thank him for the fact that he was taking an afternoon away from his demanding job at *Time* magazine to come along with me. What I *did* say was "Christ, look at that goddamn traffic." It just happens to be true that traffic in Tokyo on a business day makes Times Square look like a deserted country lane, and it was only when Mr. Chang, hearing my tone, asked me solicitously if I was feeling all right that I realized that my manners left something to be desired. Here were all these extraordinarily nice people whose time I was imposing upon, allowing themselves to be badgered into discussing subjects they'd rather not talk about. I said I felt just fine, and by the time we had snaked our way through the clogged-up streets and drawn up in front of the official building which houses the National Police Agency offices, I had recovered what passes for good humor with me in the summertime.

Official buildings seem to me to be designed by the same architects in every country, like airports. They have huge, domed lobbies, usually decorated with meaningful ceiling or wall murals, and worn marble floors which are scuffed and scarred, and overall there is a musty smell which is commingled with disinfectant. The impression I had when I entered this lobby was that it was just like the city buildings in downtown Manhattan, up to and including the chatter of hundreds of voices of secretaries and clerks and police officers milling around the lobby or crowding themselves into the elevators. The difference was that I couldn't understand what they were saying, but of course, they couldn't understand me either, and I drew some pretty curious looks since I was definitely off the beaten tourist path.

Mr. Nakahira was waiting for us in the corridor, which was painted in standard institutional washed-out green, and after the introductions and bows, he took us into the office, where everything stopped being standard institutional from my point of view. Instead of the desk and hard wooden chairs and files which I would have expected in downtown Manhattan, there were sofas and leather chairs and a coffee table. The sofas were slip-covered in cool-looking white linen, and when I had seated myself on one of them, a police officer came in with the inevitable tipple, a pot of steaming hot green tea. If Mr. Nakahira felt any reluctance about my being there, it certainly didn't show. Once he had made up his mind to see me, he could not have been more cordial or cooperative and I was thoroughly ashamed of myself for any unkind thoughts which had passed through my mind before I got there.

I was happy to be able to tell him with absolute honesty that the lack of street crime for which Japan is noted is greatly envied in our country, and that the then mayor of New York, John Lindsay, had returned from his visit to Japan full of praise for the efficiency and honesty of the police and had given a lengthy interview to the press on the subject. Mr. Nakahira accepted these compliments with a shrug of his shoulders and said, "Street crime, perhaps yes, we do a fairly good job of that, but as you well know, the *yakuza* are an entirely different matter. That does not require just good police work. It takes the cooperation of many other elements of society to uproot gangsterism, and that is not a cut-and-dried matter." (It is certainly true, of course, that street crime in our country is not a mafia activity either. Maybe that's one of the reasons why we have tolerated the mafia for so long. At least they don't mug us in the park!)

I sipped my tea and asked him what headway they actually had made in coping with the problem, and he told me with some pride that the police had managed to reduce the total number of gangsters from the one hundred fifty thousand figure I had been given to one hundred twenty-four thousand, and the number of gangs from its peak figure of five thousand to two thousand five hundred. I decided not to bring up the points which had been made to me by others, journalists, *yakuza* and *yakuza*-watchers, that breaking up ·a gang doesn't mean putting gangsters out of circulation—that they simply reform under new auspices. Nor does sending gangsters up for a term in prison spell the end of their careers necessarily—although it has been known to happen. (An ex-*yakuza* I know, one with only nine fingers, learned something about the textile trade while he was in jail, and I was told he has made a tidy sum since he came out as a manufacturer of body-shirts which are printed with *yakuza* tattoos!) That is not the general behavior pattern of released convicts, however, and I don't suppose that is a secret from the police, even if they didn't say so to me. One can scarcely blame them for emphasizing the positive, for it is clear that they have an uphill struggle on their hands. Mr. Nakahira told me that they are working on psychological as well as practical levels, trying to do a job of educating the public to regard the *yakuza* for what they are—thieves and murderers—instead of as romantic figures. They are holding seminars all over the country with community leaders in a grass-roots program, and while they don't expect any overnight miracles, they feel it is having some effect.

I felt that even the police figure of two thousand five hundred gangs is pretty awesome, and I asked Mr. Nakahira if he could give me some kind of breakdown of who they were and what they did. He was up like a shot, leaned his head into an adjoining office, and a few minutes later an officer came back with an armload of files which he put down on the coffee table. Mr. Nakahira took a pad and pencil and drew me a chart, checking through the files for reference as he did so. "You must remember," he told me (through Mr. Chang, of course), "that not all gangs are of the dimension of the Yamaguchi-gumi. Some of them have as few as twenty to thirty members, but what Taoka has succeeded in doing is to amalgamate so many of these gangs and make them the ribs which form the umbrella which he holds. There are nine such umbrellas on which we keep our eyes, and they account for all twenty-five hundred of the smaller gangs." His chart was finished and he showed it to me. It was the makeup of the Yamaguchi-gumi as of 1973.

Taoka was up there in the box on top, and under that were branches leading down to about eighty other boxes, give or take a few, which represented the major groups under his direct control, each containing the name of a sub-*oyabun* and the approximate number of people in the group—in all a conglomerate so well organized as to earn the respect of legitimate counterparts.

I asked Mr. Nakahira if he had any idea of the total annual income of the mobs, and he smiled a weary smile. "We did manage to break up one of these mobs," he said, pointing to one of the boxes on the chart, "so at least we learned what they had earned in the month in which we disbanded them. They were a gambling gang, and they had taken in somewhere between two hundred forty thousand and two hundred sixty thousand dollars. That was for one *month*, you understand."

"And how much of that," I asked, "goes to Taoka?"

"Ten percent right off the top," was the reply. I had remembered reading that Taoka had said of the Yamaguchi-gumi, "We are simply a friendship organization," and I thought to myself that it sounded like a very nice friendship offering.

Some time after my visit with Mr. Nakahira, the police released some figures on estimated annual income from gang activities. "Estimated" is the cue word, since they cannot check with any degree of accuracy their real incomes. They say it is over the one hundred thirty billion yen mark, of which the lion's share goes to the Yamaguchi-gumi, and that it comes from the marketing of narcotics, stimulants, pornographic films, gambling, extortion and other unlawful acts. The marketing of narcotics surpassed gambling for the first time as the front runner for making money. I was greatly surprised by this, since I had been told that the drug problem in Japan was practically nonexistent, but it seems that drug sales included heroin and LSD as well as marijuana and various pep pills.

Mr. Nakahira told me the names of some of the other conglomerates, and while most of them bore the names of their leaders or founders, there were some which held particular interest for me because of their political flavor. One, for instance, called the Great Japan Peace Society, another called the Japan Ultranationalist Association and another called the Japan Party of the Public-Spirited. I heard too that some of those with less militant names, such as the Inagawa-kai, led by Kakuji Inagawa, and the Tosei-kai were similarly right-wing-oriented and very active in politicking for nationalist causes. I decided to try to find out as much about that as I could at a future opportunity, but what interested me at the moment was the news about drugs as such a great source of revenue.

Taoka has gotten himself a lot of publicity with an antidrug stand. He has issued proclamations to the effect that the Yamaguchi-gumi would devote its efforts to that end, and has threatened punishment to any of his members caught trafficking in the stuff. I mentioned this to Mr. Nakahira and got a cynical "Ha!" in return. He pointed out to me that the drug traffic could not possibly have grown without Taoka's knowledge and/or participation. For one thing, the drug trade requires tremendous amounts of capital investment, the sort of thing which the Yamaguchi-gumi could underwrite without a quiver. The Awakening Drug Control Law of 1972 is stiff, and the risk of getting caught and being imprisoned for many years is very high. Addicts and smugglers are extremely careful to deal only with known criminals who can be easily identified as gangsters, rather than with someone who might be an informer or a police agent. Those who were rounded up by the police in one year turned out to be chiefly members of the Sumiyoshi family and the Inagawa-kai, both of which have brotherhood relationships with the Yamaguchi-gumi, so Mr. Nakahira's "Ha!" really means something. It was also pointed out to me that the underworld bosses have met in secret to fix the street price of stimulants, and they think it highly unlikely that such meetings would pass unnoticed by Taoka, as they involved his own lieutenants.

On the subject of drugs, the police of Japan, while their job is tough enough, would seem not to be in quite the same league with that of our police, for drug traffic

is still very much contained within the ranks of organized crime. There are no free-lance street pushers
hanging around the schools and parks. According to
police officials, drugs are sold to customers at gambling
sessions in order to keep them awake through the
night-long sessions, thus upping their banker's fees,
and to make addicts of prostitutes under their control.
There is also a fast set of swingers who are not *yakuza*
and are drug-users. And drugs are in big demand from
gangsters themselves who have night-shift assignments
as employees of bars, clubs and massage parlors, or as
truck and taxi drivers. I did ask some young women
students whom I know whether there was any around
in their crowd. They said yes, there was lots of hashish
if you knew the right people, and somebody usually did.
They are extremely careful about their use of marijuana
and hashish, as possession is punishable by very harsh
penalties if they are caught.

The Awakening Drug Control Law of 1972 had come
as a result of the seizure of huge quantities of hashish
and marijuana from a ring operating in Tokyo. (The
roundup of this ring turned up quite a few Americans,
incidentally, including one U.S. Air Force medical
officer, who served as suppliers to Japanese gangsters.)
This group and others to which the police were led
were manufacturing marijuana-cum-heroin-powder
cigarettes, and the police and public were properly ter-
rified that this could herald a revival of what they
termed the "nightmarish heroin age," which the Japanese had seemed to lick some years earlier. At present
there is a maximum ten-year jail sentence and a fine of
five hundred thousand yen for illicit sale, possession or
use of stimulants, and now the authorities are pressing

for laws which will be even stiffer. I hope they get them. There is not, incidentally, a single instance of police corruption such as that in the notorious "French Connection" case, where police officers got rich on what they stole and sold.

I think I wanted to believe that Taoka was sincere in personally deploring the drug traffic, but the police looked at me as though I had two heads when I asked in a small voice, wasn't it *possible?* I heard about a rash of violence and shoot-outs which had occurred throughout areas of high gangster activity to control the territory for the marketing of pep pills. Did I, could I possibly believe that such things went on behind Taoka's back?

The tea had gotten cold and since nobody had come in to replenish the pot, it dawned on me that I had used up enough of the police department's time, so I gathered up the various research reports and dossiers which they had given me and prepared to take my leave. Mr. Nakahira had been extremely kind and patient with me, and now he said, "They're not knights in armor, you know. Don't believe whatever you see at the movies about our *yakuza.*" The message was clear. The police view is that *giri, ninjo, jingi,* all the phrases which I had been hearing, the high-flown prose which *yakuza* are given to in describing themselves and which are the delight of film-makers and drooling fans, are not what it's all about. The name of the game, they say, is M-O-N-E-Y, and all the tattoos and kimonos and decorated samurai swords will not change one letter of it.

Mr. Nakahira's suggestion that it would take the co-operation of "other elements of society" left me with the distinct impression that he wasn't getting it. Japanese gangsters, it would appear, are not only well organized, they are well connected.

A few years ago the public was astonished to learn that their former prime minister Nobosuke Kishi, their former education minister Umekichi Nakamura, and an LDP Diet man named Shuji Kurauchi had gone bail for a Yamaguchi-gumi member who had been indicted for murder. The public was similarly shocked by the news that a former cabinet member had sent an elaborate wreath to the funeral of a leading underworld figure. Such incidents are straws in the wind, but there seemed to be enough of them to point to a much deeper involvement, and to bear out the contention of sociologists that gangsters serve the function of helping those in power to maintain it.

Those in power would certainly include the business community, and as I've mentioned, the *yakuza* are enthusiastic helpers in the mission to prevent strong labor unions from forming. But they supply another service which is, I believe, unique in the annals of crime. I don't mean it to sound frivolous, but when I heard it described, it sounded exactly like a dial-a-gangster service, and the companies which use it can argue that it's not even illegal. Perhaps not laudable, but legal. You'd use this service if your company was due to have a stockholders' meeting that you wanted to go off without a hitch. You figure you've been running things just fine, prospering mightily, making lots of money for the company and the shareholders, and what have they got to kick about? It's a nuisance to have to be accountable to them, to have to explain your policies such as why a little pollution isn't such a terrible thing after all, but that's part of your corporate duty and there's no escaping it. To avoid answering a lot of embarrassing or damnfool questions from people who don't know anything about running a company, you pick up the phone and call the *sokaiya,* which means "general-meeting experts." This idea is a new gimmick which gangsters have hit upon to increase their income.

The service the *sokaiya* render is to send around a lot of plug-uglies who will ring the auditorium where the meeting is taking place with their arms folded across their chests, just scowling and looking sinister. As a rule, that is all they will be required to do because what they are actually capable of doing is so well known that every meeting is a model of serenity, full of peaceful agreement to the proposals of the executive board, and seldom lasts more than fifteen minutes. Of course, if some ill-advised stockholder is foolish enough to question a policy, the *sokaiya* can scarcely be blamed for hustling the agitator out and beating him black and blue—that's what they're there for. And precisely that has been known to happen. There was a meeting, for instance, of Mitsubishi Heavy Industry stockholders (reported by Mr. Chang in *Time* magazine) where a group of peace advocates protested Mitsubishi's arms production. True, they had purchased shares in the company for exactly that purpose, so how convenient that the *sokaiya* just happened to be on hand to break a few legs and arms! Even the powerful Mitsubishi could not risk the public loss of face that would be involved if they admitted having invited them, and every executive who was questioned about the event answered by saying in effect, "Who me? Uh-uh! Wouldn't think of it!" Well, everybody knows what great patriots the *yakuza* are, so maybe they simply arrived spontaneously.

If Mr. Nakahira is stymied by the fact that big business refuses to cooperate with the police in the matter of *sokaiya*, his frustration is even greater in another area which involves gangster connections with business—blackmail and extortion. Opening the doors to gangsters in industry has been for them like inviting a snake into the house. As company spies and general-meeting experts, the gangsters have used their "in" status to amass bits and pieces of information which might cause embarrassment or worse to the company or to an executive, or which might lend itself at best to dubious interpretation. In this activity, the *yakuza*, being themselves Japanese, understand exactly how far their victims will go to protect the company's or their own image. Fortunately they have overestimated in a few instances, and a handful of beleaguered pigeons who were squeezed beyond endurance brought themselves to go to the police. There's no way to check how many companies and individuals have been victimized in this manner, but a few cases are known.

The name Michio Sasaki has appeared earlier. He is a Taoka lieutenant and an *oyabun* in his own right, and he went into the shakedown business in a big way. Before the police caught up with him he had been doing a thriving business in blackmail, and the two operations on which they nailed him netted him one hundred thousand dollars from one corporation and sixteen thousand dollars from a Tokyo bank which finally decided to turn him in because his insistent demands for further payment, which looked as though they would never end, threatened to close them down eventually. Sasaki

was only put away for a while, but he could afford to sit
back patiently and smile because of the number of cases
which had not come to light. What he had on them was
knowledge of some slightly irregular deals, such as
loans without proper security, investments without
proper notification to stockholders, that sort of thing.
But before they caved in at the knees and sent for the
cops, it was a common sight to see Sasaki living it up at
expensive restaurants with nervous executives and a
few sumo wrestlers whom he brought along for color
and perhaps just in case.

Sasaki's arrest had an epilogue. Among those who do
not admire the *yakuza* or see anything romantic about
their shenanigans are the members of the press. Mr.
Chang's story in *Time* included the information that the
Yomiuri Shimbun, one of Japan's largest dailies, is a case
in point. They did a feature story on the Sasaki clan in
which they referred to them as a "pack of bandits,"
thereby arousing some very hurt feelings at clan headquarters. They decided to teach the paper a lesson by
sending an attack unit to stage a daylight raid on the
newspaper's Osaka city room. They broke in "howling
like mad dogs" an eyewitness says, armed with steel
bars, and as they screamed some expletives, they
smashed desks and windows and files and beat up
eleven editorial writers. The only word I can think of to
describe the tender, hurt feelings of the *yakuza* which
resulted in this escapade is *chutzpah,* which has been
translated from the Yiddish to mean the sort of gall it
takes to murder your mother and father and then plead
for clemency on the grounds that you are an orphan.

Sasaki has established himself as a kingpin among
blackmailers, but he is by no means the only one who

has gone into the business. The police estimate that millions, perhaps billions, of yen are collected by the *yakuza* through this practice, cases which never come to light. One gang of blackmailers which the police *were* able to round up in Tokyo, as recently reported in the *Daily Yomiuri*, was something called the Gokokudan, which translates as the Society for Defense of the Fatherland, and which is actually registered as a right-wing political organization. It's difficult to see in precisely what way they were defending the fatherland by extorting fifty million yen of stock certificates and bank checks from two housing lot developers.

The methods used for this extortion were rather medieval. They kept the developers blindfolded and gagged at "political" headquarters for two weeks, beating them regularly with oak staves, according to the police spokesman. The arrested men explained their behavior by saying that the beatings were in retaliation for the fact that they had loaned the developers twenty million yen and the developers had not met the date for repayment. The additional thirty million yen which they extorted was to punish them.

The police investigation went further into the Gokokudan, and they learned that they had extorted ten million yen from a big-time construction contractor, five million from another, and twenty million from a taxi company, and that they had also defended the fatherland by running regularly scheduled gambling sessions in a metropolitan government-operated apartment. But for every Gokokudan which comes to light through excesses in their behavior toward their victims, there are dozens which manage to stay under cover discreetly, applying pressure where it hurts, but not so much that their victims will risk public exposure by calling the police. It's nice to have a racket where your dupes are so pathetically, endearingly anxious to protect you from prosecution that they refuse to lodge complaints against you.

In the run-of-the-mill gangster activities such as prostitution, drug-trafficking, gambling and so on, the police are more easily able to declare war and occasionally win a skirmish if not the entire battle. In those which are more complicated and which involve powerful figures in the political and business communities, however, they virtually have their hands tied. Not that they have given up by any means, for they have been working in another direction through which they hope to put a good number of big shots behind bars. They have borrowed a leaf from our own crime history when the FBI and the tax people got together to prosecute Al Capone and others on tax evasion, all other means having failed. The National Police Agency is now working with the National Tax Agency on the returns of Kazuo Taoka and a handful of others. Still, putting some gangsters away and getting rid of gangsterism are two different things, as the police well know, and that will not disappear until the police are able to count on what they ask for—the cooperation of the society as a whole.

To My Dearest
Florence

Jiro Tamiya

Jiro Tamiya in *Theatre of Life*, a *yakuza* film.

Tattooed yakuza.
(Bernard Krisher, Newsweek)

CHAPTER II

MR. NAKAHIRA'S closing re-
marks to me not to believe everything I saw in the
movies sent me, of course, to the movies. I had understood his point—that it is demonstrably harder to teach
people that gangsters are villains when a popular
propaganda mill keeps picturing them as heroes—and
I had another reason. Mitsuru Taoka was at the time
producing his first film, a glorified version of his father's early days along the waterfront. The police were
at their wit's end trying to prevent it from being made.
They forbade, they got injunctions, they issued state-
ments in the press, trying to get the public to make an

organized protest, to no avail. Mitsuru-san had told me of the delays in production, and when I asked him whether he thought the police would succeed in their efforts to halt production, he smiled. "No way," he said. "We'll finish this picture, you can bet on it. There's too much money involved, and how can they stop us? What law are we breaking?"

He was right. They finished it, distributed it, and it was an enormous success, starring as it did the king of *yakuza* films, Ken Takakura, who's a lot prettier than Taoka. The picture was shot at Toei studio, which seems to have many friends in high places who can be called upon to see that nothing interferes with production.

I rounded up a friend of mine named Isao-san, who is in show business, and who I know is a gangster-film buff, and at ten o'clock on a Saturday morning we went to an art film house in the Ginza. We could have gone at three or four o'clock in the morning just as well, because on weekends, houses which specialize in these *yakuza-eiga,* as they are called, show them around the clock. The audience, not just the makeup but the size, interested me almost as much as the films. They packed the theater to the rafters, even at that ungodly hour for movie-going, and even though the rest of Tokyo seemed to have emptied out for the weekend. That's the whole point of making *yakuza-eiga.* Not to frustrate the police, but to make money. Crime, the movie-makers have learned, does pay—very handsomely. Were it not for the *yakuza-eiga* and those sexy little comedies they grind out, the movie industry of Japan would go broke. The legitimate movie industry, that is. The porno films which are made and marketed by *yakuza* are another matter.

The *yakuza-eiga* have achieved the status of art films in certain circles. Not being a movie critic myself, I'm not sure what that means, but many esteemed writers (the late Yukio Mishima, for instance, whose gory suicide, *seppuku,* slitting his own belly right to left, then decapitation by a confederate, matched anything the writers of *yakuza-eiga* ever dreamed up) have written long, learned articles in praise of them. I yield to their superior critical eyes, but I'm afraid I have a blind spot about what constitutes art in a film. It's not that I don't enjoy *yakuza-eiga* in the same way that I enjoyed the old-time westerns, the kind they made before they got "meaningful." The style is broad and you can tell the good guys from the bad guys not by the white and black hats, but by the noble looks, the grim determination, the inner struggle mirrored in their faces, the furious reaction to injustice. If underplaying is your dish, the *yakuza-eiga* are not for you, although there are a few extraordinary actors who play in them. As in the westerns, there are certain obligatory characters and obligatory scenes:

There is a good *oyabun* and a bad *oyabun.* The good *oyabun* is motivated by humanitarian feelings, the bad *oyabun* is merely greedy and wishes to take over. There is a *yakuza* woman, sometimes a geisha, sometimes a harlot with a heart of gold, sometimes a gambling accomplice. There is a gambling scene where somebody cheats, is discovered, the kimonos are dropped from the shoulders revealing tattoos (cheers from the audience), swords appear and blood is spilled. These scenes, red ink, ketchup or no, are unbelievably sick-making, but the audience can hardly wait for them. There's one scene I like, where gangsters introduce themselves in a special *yakuza* argot which most people think is slang, but which a scholar informed me is actually a form of archaic Japanese, comparable to medieval English. The audience waits for these scenes as ours do for the long walk and the fast draw.

The *yakuza-eiga* give short shrift to a non-*yakuza* population which presumably exists in limbo some place, and this is very much in keeping with the real-life *yakuza* propaganda that they live in a world of their own, never overstepping the boundaries. If this was true in the past, it certainly is not true now, but then the *yakuza-eiga* are mostly laid in the past. It is only within the past few years that they have begun to make some films with more modern backgrounds.

Whatever the artistic merits of these films, it is really the morality expressed that deserves attention, for most of them are, to use a word I've been trying to avoid, fascist in their outlook. They place their highest emphasis on duty to a cause over every other consideration, never mind whether the cause is in itself admirable. They exalt regimentation and suppress opposition, to say nothing of the fact that their attitude toward my sex is nothing less than archaic! We may be dear lovable creatures who drive men mad and all that, but we're definitely inferior in these films. That attitude goes for real-life *yakuza* too. According to Koji Kata, the ex-*yakuza* turned writer, the *yakuza* have a male-chauvinist attitude toward women, and they express it in their slogan, "Be a man, live like a man," which stems from the feudal attitudes of old Japan.

In this as in other attitudes, the *yakuza* are not in step with the changing patterns of modern Japan. There the status of women has shown symptoms of progress in the past few years, although from the American point of view it may still leave much to be desired. Girls of good family are turning up in business, not just as clerks and typists but as executives here and there; many have begun to date boys and pick out their own husbands; they have become involved in political and civil rights movements and all sorts of things which only ten years ago would have seemed impossible. I don't wish to give the impression that this is widespread or even general, but it is happening and in my own opinion once that sort of thing starts, there's no stopping it. I hope. Where it's not happening is among the *yakuza*, comfortable old traditionalists that they are.

Now, about the movie audience. In societies like our own and that of the Japanese, where industrialization, mechanization and more and more laws restricting our personal behavior are enacted, it is inevitable, I suppose, that legends around outlaw heroes should grow. The man who lives by his wits and is a law unto himself plays right into our fantasies and gives us a chance to get rid of our aggressive feelings in our tightly regulated societies. If you kept your eyes closed and didn't understand a word of Japanese, you'd know the exact moment in the film when somebody takes the law into his own hands because of the Go! Go! Go! attitude of the audience.

Lots of *yakuza* attend these movies, and why not? The films strengthen their self-image, and besides it's nice to see the public cheering for you for a change. Lots of young people too, kids who go just for kicks in some instances. And others who Japanese psychologists say go to find that "altruistic purity" which they attach to *yakuza* heroes. One of the psychologists, Hitoshi Aiba, says that "young people in Japan have no faith in their future. They think everything is fixed, and they go to the films so that they can imagine they are like the *yakuza,* breaking out of the establishment." "They are indoctrinated from childhood," according to Noboru Ando, who used to be a *yakuza* himself and is now an actor, "with the belief that the group is more important than the individual. No wonder they like to watch men who have the courage to do things alone," says Ando. It's a total fraud, of course. The *yakuza* no more act alone than does anyone else. They act on instructions of the *oyabun,* and just because it's counter-establishment doesn't make it the less regimented behavior.

The young audience which interested me the most were the students, those of the radical left and of the radical right. The latter I can understand, but as to the former, it's hard to see how they identify with a body of men who are dedicated to their overthrow, except on the general terms that anyone who works against the establishment for *whatever* reason can't be all bad. It has also been stated that youth of both political wings have studied these films and made notes from them on how to cope with authority in the event of confrontation. I personally think that's hogwash, having seen upward of two dozen of these films. They can learn a lot more from their underground press.

It was no surprise to me to learn that the *yakuza* themselves are big fans of *yakuza-eiga* for, as I said, they bolster their self-image. It should be remembered that

the average rank-and-file *yakuza* is no Taoka, living in
luxury with chauffeured cars, bodyguards, estates. He's
more likely a cheap grifter or a petty hood, doing the
bread-and-butter work which has to be done to rake in
those billions of yen which keep the gangs solvent. He's
a smuggler, a gambler, a gunman, an extortionist, a
pimp, and his share of the take, whatever he does, may
not be much more than he'd have earned in his father's
noodle shop if he'd stayed home like a good boy. He's
no charismatic boss commanding an empire. He's just
another punk, sitting around some dive in Shinjuku
with a couple of buddies most of the time, all of them
dressed in flared pants, oversized loose jackets, under
which they're wearing wide belly-warming belts, handy
for tucking in knives, and pointed shoes or sandals.
Sure it's a costume. The wearer wants you to recognize
that he's a *yakuza*. It's all he has, and to him it's a lot.
Of course, he can dream of working his way up the
ladder in *yakuza* circles, but considering his equipment
(low IQ according to police research, poor education
and family background), it's not likely to happen.

But he likes being able to put on a ceremonial
kimono from time to time and be part of a great, mysti-
cal organization, and to use his gang connections to
swagger into cafes, maybe sit down with a celebrity such
as a sumo wrestler or a pop singer, or hang around the
racetrack or at strip-tease joints and bars where he
might get some drinks and sex on the house. Belonging
is the most important consideration, more even than
money. Sociologist Chie Nakane speaks of the "frame"
which is so important to every Japanese, and which she
defines as "a locality, an institution or a particular relationship which binds a set of individuals into one

group." Taoka has created a frame for his *kobun* for he remembers how desperately he himself sought one. It is cemented with rituals and argot and most important of all, loyalty to him. Within that frame they have hosts of brothers and a strong father. Outside of it they have nothing, and there aren't many *yakuza* who would be brave enough to jeopardize their standing within the frame by getting out of line, since ostracism is more to be dreaded even than loss of life. They are happy and eager to conform to their group ethic and mores. There is even a Japanese proverb which goes, "The nail that sticks up must be hammered down." They believe in that.

And withal, despite the killings and the violence and the knavery, they see themselves as the heroes of those *yakuza-eiga.* One of those documents which came from the police was the survey I just mentioned, done by the Police Research Institute. It was conducted among *yakuza,* and it revealed a self-image which only Sir Galahad could live up to. A *yakuza,* was the consensus among *yakuza,* must be first of all powerful and muscular. He must be brave, generous, sympathetic and amicable. He must have guts and leadership qualities, and be prepared to use action instead of words. He must know his place and live by *giri.* And of course, he must be smart. No wonder he likes the films. That's just the way the *yakuza* come off.

There is another example of the shrewd psychological means which Taoka has used to bind his *kobun* together in the Yamaguchi-gumi. A certain loss of the personal quality could have been expected in their vast expansion, but Taoka is a bit of a genius, and he hit upon the idea of a house organ, a notion which, while certainly in the cherished tradition of big business, is not precisely what you would expect in gangland.

The paper is called the *Yamaguchi-gumi Jiho,* and it's really more of a magazine than a newspaper. Nor is it any underground publication run off in the dead of night in somebody's cellar on a duplicating machine. It's a very slick, four-color job intended for internal distribution, but when you consider that in addition to the thousands of Yamaguchi-gumi members, there are a hundred fifty thousand *yakuza* in Japan who might well be interested in the contents, that's not such bad circulation. The cover could be the Yamaguchi gumi flag against the background of a globe (makes you think, doesn't it?) or perhaps crossed with the flag of Japan, and the contents include articles which have a wide range of interest.

There are canons and precepts laid down in the pages for the guidance of the membership which are lofty enough to have been composed by a churchman, and which very well may be, for that matter. There are also minutes of meetings held by members in which they discussed such matters as the awful prejudiced mass media and its leftish propaganda. They run a serial, a *yakuza* soap opera, dealing with Japanese gang history, loaded with instances of *giri* and *ninjo;* there is usually an essay on chivalry, and there are columns with Social Notes from All Over such as who's just come out of jail, who's just going in, who got married, who died, who was blessed with a son or (ugh) a daughter—the same sort of thing you'd find in any newspaper. There's also a sports section with heavy emphasis on sumo wrestling, naturally, since they are so deeply involved in it, and scores of golf games in their own gangster tournaments. There are in addition poems and articles on criminal law (what else?).

There are also theater and movie reviews, with a lot of professionalism going into the critique of *yakuza* films. There was a rave, not surprisingly, for the one which dealt with the early days of Taoka's life. Special pleading perhaps, but other newspapers also gave it good reviews.

Incidentally, I should like to make the point that although *yakuza* involvement in the running of some studios certainly exists, and there are *yakuza* and ex-*yakuza* and *yakuza*-connected people who play and direct some of these films, there are many, many more which are made by people with no such involvement. They do them without sinister motives, unless you happen to feel that making money is a nefarious occupation. They do these films because they feel they're good yarns, they know the audience loves them, and they could argue as do some psychologists that they furnish a harmless outlet for aggression. If the police don't happen to see them that way, it can't be helped. But one of these movie-makers did admit to me that he didn't blame the police for making a to-do about the Taoka film. To glorify a living gangster—the first time in film history in Japan that this has been done—seemed to him to be actually counterproductive, for it could create a feeling of antipathy for the whole genre. It didn't, as it happens, but as my friend said, "I know Taoka and I sort of like him, but I don't think he's a very good example to show to our young people. If you quote me, don't mention my name."

CHAPTER 12

BANZUIIN CHOBEI, the swaggering ex-samurai, was the ideal *yakuza* for feudal Japan, motivated by passion, by *giri* and *ninjo*. Kazuo Taoka, for all that he professes to have taken Banzuiin as his model, resembles much more closely a twentieth-century chairman of the board. Thoroughly corporate minded, he did what the head of any giant conglomerate would do: he moved into one territory after another, swallowing up the weaker competition along the way with a display of greater strength and greater organization. Once he had learned to hold his violence in check, he proved capable of bending with the wind, of making compromises with *gurentai* and *sangokujin* and formerly hated rivals in other gangs, all in the interest of building the corporation. By the early 1960s he had brought himself up by the bootstraps from a waterfront hoodlum to the most powerful *yakuza oyabun* in the Kansai area, leader of the biggest gang in Japan.

All right, I told myself, in some ways they only seem different from our mafia. Some of the customs—kimonos, tattoos, swords, *giri-ninjo,* finger-cutting—all of these seemed exotic and strange to me, but no more so than *omertà,* vein-slitting, oath-taking and other mafia rituals might seem to a Japanese. Deep down, I had concluded, prostitution is prostitution, gambling is gambling, loan sharks are loan sharks, drug-peddling is drug-peddling and so on. Whether it's done by the mafia or the *yakuza,* in five-hundred-buck suits or kimonos, their capital gains are accumulated through serving the ills and vices of the societies in which they function. They're just the same, I said, and up to a point I was right. But only up to a point, and if Taoka had been content to consolidate his gains and stay in Kansai, I'd never have learned about the area in which they depart from the regular gangster pattern and become something rather more frightening from my point of view.

They are an integral part of an ultranationalist, extremist right-wing grouping of elements from the business and academic communities (with even some members from the religious community) who have as their aim "turning Japan back to traditional values" and "preventing a communist takeover." The usefulness of well-disciplined, well-armed *yakuza* in these jingoistic circles seems obvious. Ideologically they belong in such an amalgam, but recruiting them was the brain child of

Yoshio Kodama, to whom the newspapers refer as "godfather of the right." In seeking information about *yakuza*, the name of Kodama kept coming up, and originally I had been amazed to learn that he was not a *yakuza* at all. "Unless," as Richard Halloran told me when I inquired about him, "you think of everyone who doesn't see eye-to-eye with you as a gangster. Kodama's *connections* are very interesting just the same."

So they are. And I only found out about them because of Taoka's dream of invading the Kanto area and making his Yamaguchi-gumi the all-Japan Yamaguchi-gumi. For that he needed political influence as well as muscle and guile, and Kodama was the logical person to supply it.

Ties between the mafia and the machines which run most American cities have always been notorious—and denied by all parties involved. Crime commissions such as the Kefauver Committee and crusading journalists have periodically exposed unsavory tie-ups in high places, but the collaborations have always been conducted on a furtive level and vigorously disavowed when they were brought to light, with howls of persecution and frame-up filling the air. And informants have spoken of multi-million-dollar slush funds maintained by the mafia as a regular operating overhead expense for the corruption of law-enforcement officers and the election of complaisant officials. In Japan, where such ties exist, they are openly acknowledged and their base is an ideological one—that handy old expedient which even *yakuza* haters cannot object to, anti-communism.

Skilled though he is in the manipulation of *yakuza* criminal activities, when it comes to politics, Kazuo

Taoka is a babe in arms compared to Yoshio Kodama. Kodama even looks more like a gangster than Taoka. He is built like an ex-pug, stocky and muscular; his hair is so closely cropped as to make him seem bald; his square face has a broad, flat nose, a full, rather sensuous mouth, and narrowed, reptilian eyes. He is absolutely perfect type-casting for a *yakuza,* but he is only a fellow traveler. Or vice versa. Actually, he marks the route.

At this stage of his life, Kodama is not happy when the press call him the "godfather of the right." Even as far back as 1956 he was trying to shake loose of that label.

"Nonsense," he told one reporter for the *Yomiuri Japan News,* "I am not an ultranationalist or professional rightist. I find that embarrassing and downright annoying. Such people are eccentrics, living in a dream. Their homes are festooned with straw and paper symbols on altars, and when you talk to them they make no sense."

That is the mellow statement of a seasoned battler who has turned his back on the hotheaded tactics of his youth, but if he isn't a professional rightist, he'll do until one comes along. To bolster up his claim that he is no fanatic, he points to the fact that he was never a member of such ultranationalist societies as the Black Dragon, but he leaves out the fact that as a young man his firebrand activities got him arrested several times, once when he dramatically attempted to approach the Emperor directly to inveigh against the formation of a political party which he considered to be leftist, the New Labor-Farmer Party. He was just the same age at the time he started his inflammatory right-wing politicking as Taoka was when he was arrested the first time for murder, but his background was quite different. He was not a child of privilege, having come from a lower-middle-class family, but he was a university student, involved with intellectuals rather than with hooligans.

Kodama began to come into his own at the precise time that Taoka was beginning his self-education by reading political history in jail. Kodama seemed to have an extraordinary talent for organizing and for finance, and the military build-up in Japan had use for men with such talent. He was no longer regarded as a right-wing fanatic—his thinking was now in the mainstream of the men who were running the country.

Fortuitously, or perhaps because he had friends in high places who could keep him advised of the progress of events, he organized something called the Kodama Organization, just a little bit in advance of Pearl Harbor. Its purpose was to procure war materiel for Naval Air Headquarters. They purchased supplies outside the country and paid for them, as Mr. Kodama says, "fairly and squarely." He doesn't say what he charged the Japanese Navy for them, but it's fair to assume that patriotism or no patriotism, as the war years went on and many materials grew scarce, the Kodama Organization didn't suffer. In that same interview quoted above, he himself said that his organization grew like a colossus.

At the end of the war, communist China confiscated the factories which he had built outside the country and the vessels which he had used for shipping—the total worth of which he estimates as having been well in excess of a billion yen, but he still had a hefty little nest egg to play around with which he had managed to secrete, the equivalent of about three and a half million dollars.

When the war ended, the straggling and discredited elements of ultranationalism were struggling to maintain a power base so that they could emerge at some future, more propitious time. With Kodama's record— a total of seven years spent in jail for extremist activities —it was not surprising that he was regarded as a Class A war criminal whose efforts had helped to bring Japan into a disastrous war, and he was arrested. But even if he was going to jail, his money wasn't, and a behind-the-scenes manipulator in political circles named Tsuji approached him to turn over his fortune to help finance a new, genuinely conservative party. Kodama had realistically assessed the bitterness abroad in the land toward those who had urged a war on them, and he knew he was not beloved by the U.S. military occupying authorities, so he considered the possibility that he might never get out of jail. He therefore entrusted Tsuji with his property, with the stipulation that whatever else the party he formed was to stand for, it must firmly uphold the emperor system. Not necessarily the emperor as the head of state, but at least as the symbol. There were others he had in mind to be the actual head. The party which Tsuji used Kodama's money to found was the present Liberal-Democratic Party, although Kodama at this date feels the ruling clique of the party has become decadent.

As with Taoka, Kodama spent his time in jail planning for his future. In that same *Yomiuri* interview he said, "Leading a dreary life, loafing around Sugamo prison in nothing more than a loincloth during the summer months, I woke up to myself. I realized that I might as well take it easy after I got out of jail, rather than be thrown into jail for living up to my convictions." What he meant by "taking it easy" was that there wasn't much percentage in being taken out of circulation periodically. He would have to play it cautiously if he were to devote his life to nationalist causes, for people did not really seem to understand genuine nationalism. A false step and his plan could be crushed by the people and the government before it got under way. Let others lead the marches and carry the banners. With his brains and money, he could see to it that there were plenty of marchers without himself having to join the parade and get his head bashed in, figuratively and literally. Though *he* had changed no opinions he had held before the war, the country as a whole was sick of the kind of thinking which had led them into a holocaust. There were still those who felt as he did, he knew, and he planned to bring them all together. Among them were other *oyabun* like Taoka, if not of his standing, and groups like the Yamaguchi-gumi whose political inclinations were in the right direction, if not so sophisticated as his own.

When he came out of jail he stuck with his resolve to remain behind the scenes, to be what the Japanese call *kuromaku* (a Kabuki theater term which means "black curtain"; it refers to those prop men who manipulate the scenery, but you're not supposed to see them because they're dressed in black). His power and influence began to grow, reaching high enough for him to be in a position to have a hand in naming prime ministers. In jail he had become the friend of a fellow convict in on the same charge, Nobosuka Kishi, who became prime minister in 1957 with Kodama's help, and before that he helped break the hold of the late Shigeru Yoshida, who had been the strongest force in postwar politics, so that he could make another friend of his, Hatoyama, the prime minister. After Kishi had served his term, he persuaded Kodama to exert his influence once again in favor of his younger brother, Eisaku Sato, which he was glad to do, and the latter became prime minister in 1964. When I learned all this, I was not surprised that everyone who had told me to find out about Kodama had urged me to proceed cautiously, that it was an extremely delicate and sensitive area, and that he had powerful allies.

But it was his efforts to amalgamate gangsters which held the greatest interest for me, and which were of paramount concern to Kazuo Taoka. Kodama's first move in this direction, in the early '6os, was to form the Kanto-kai, an organization which consisted of the six leading gangster groups in the Kanto area. They were called the Kinsei-kai, Sumiyoshi-kai, Matsuba-kai, Gi-jin-to, Tosei-kai and Hokusei-kai, and under Kodama's leadership they pledged "to unify ourselves in our resolve to dedicate our lives for the sake of the nation." They drew up a set of principles which included the following: (1) To protect and promote liberal democracy in Japan, and to fight against those who hindered the group in its pursuit. (2) To challenge communism and fight against it, and to inspire patriotism in the Japanese people. (3) To cooperate with Asian countries and promote unification of Asian countries. (4) "The Kanto-kai shall not be restricted by any group of any sort, and this group is to pursue its aim from a nationalistic point of view."

Mr. Kodama was to be congratulated in getting these rival groups to lay aside their differences for so noble a purpose, but in spite of all their fine resolves, the police files which I was permitted to read state that whatever Kodama's purpose might have been, the gangsters who came together had another purpose in mind which did not appear in their charter—to keep Kazuo Taoka out of the Kanto area. They were determined that the dreaded Yamaguchi-gumi should not invade the lush territory which included Tokyo and Yokohama, and to this end they were even willing to forget their inner warfare to unite against him. The Kinsei-kai in particular, led by a powerful *oyabun* named Kakuji Inagawa, was determined to shed all the blood it would take to keep Taoka out, and Inagawa had publicly stated, "So long as I am alive, Taoka will not set one foot into Kanto territory."

Taoka paid little attention to such bold utterances, nor had he any intention of risking men and arms in an ugly gang war. Instead of girding for battle, he approached his rightist friend, a rival to Kodama in that field, named Seigen Tanaka—the man who had been so helpful to him in his struggle for supremacy on the waterfront. Tanaka did all he could for him, introducing him to leading companies and banks in Tokyo through which he could make connections for investments, but Taoka needed more than that. He needed connections with important *yakuza* bosses whom he could seduce into helping him against Inagawa, and unfortunately Tanaka had none. Kodama, however, did, and in 1961 or 1962 Taoka finally approached him.

Kodama was delighted to meet the powerful man. The connections which Tanaka had made for Taoka

were useful to Kodama, and the Yamaguchi-gumi
would be a welcome addition to his group. Taoka's
anticommunist feeling had by now been publicly stated.
(I should add that when I spoke with the police about
this, they were extremely skeptical about his sincerity
even in that. They felt it was simply a ploy to help him
expand his territory. I'm sure there was that element
involved in his thinking, but I also think he is sincerely
anti-communist.) Taoka had also used his ideological
conviction as an excuse to invade the territory when
there was some trouble around the waterfront in Hiroshima. "As I put such great importance to the protection of harbors from communism," he had said in his
memoirs, "I could not be bothered by the death of
three or four cheap *yakuza*. They mean nothing when
we think about the future of this country. What concerns me most is the protection of harbors from communist inroads." A statement to warm the cockles of
Kodama's heart, surely, and this was evidently a man
well worth cultivating. As a result he gave Taoka the
toehold he was looking for in Kanto by arranging a
brotherhood with the Tosei-kai, one of the gangs in his
Kanto-kai. The Tosei-kai, as it happened, was a Korean
gang, headed by a notorious *yakuza* named Chong Kyu
Young, but for so important an inroad Taoka was able
to overcome his racial hostility.

The brotherhood ceremony was set up in a Japanese
restaurant in Kobe. Kodama himself invited various big
shots—non-*yakuza* from the Kanto area—to attend; and
Taoka, to impress these visiting celebrities, set up an
honorary guard of honor. One thousand Yamaguchi-
gumi members lined the streets from the railroad station at Kobe to the restaurant. The result of this new

relationship was that the Tosei-kai was boycotted by other Kanto-kai *yakuza*, and Kodama may have made one of his few tactical errors in arranging it, since the internecine warfare which ensued marked the end of the Kanto-kai.

There were a few incidents after that, between the Yamaguchi-gumi and its bitter enemy, Kakuji Inagawa's group, including the attempted murder of some of Inagawa's executives. A major war, in fact, was only averted because Kodama stepped in and acted as arbitrator, drawing up a set of proposals for peace which he presented to Taoka. They stated: (1) The Yamaguchi-gumi should expel all who had been involved in the attack. (2) The leader of the attack group should chop off his little finger and present it to Inagawa. (3) Taoka was to apologize personally to Inagawa. (4) In return for all of this, the Yamaguchi-gumi would be allowed to put ten men, but not more, into Yokohama.

Whether Taoka acceded to the first three conditions or not is not recorded, but on the last, he was not a man to sit quietly by and let others decide his fate. Once again he turned to his friend Seigen Tanaka and shook hands on a deal to set up something called the Yokohama Branch of the League for Stamping Out Drug Traffic. Moving quickly, before Inagawa or anyone else could put a spoke in his wheel, he got a large number of respectable celebrities to sit on the board, including the president of Rikkyo University, a few members of the Upper House, some writers and others —after all, who would refuse to stand up and be counted in a crusade of that nature? Without consulting anyone, he established a branch office for Yamaguchi-gumi headquarters in Yokohama, one of the richest of

the Kanto territories. Inagawa was enraged at this viola-
tion of the stipulation to allow only ten men on the
scene, and he called upon Kodama to do something
about it. When Kodama did, in fact, approach Taoka,
he replied that he would be delighted to leave
Yokohama just as soon as the narcotics problem was
thoroughly expelled from the premises. Nothing further was said.

The demise of the Kanto-kai was a small deterrent to
Kodama's ambition to unite all gangsters, but it was not
the death of his plan. He went along, building his influence in those and other areas, accumulating obligations
and debts, *giri* and *ninjo* by performing services in
which he was skilled. Tirelessly he used his money and
his talents, cultivating this one and that one, doing favors, settling disputes. He was rather like a giant pup-
peteer, pulling the right strings at the right time. When
a war loomed between the Japan Line and the Sankyo
Steamship Company, the call went out, "Get Kodama."
Kodama was happy to oblige, and he settled the matter
to everyone's satisfaction. Same thing when problems
threatened the stability of the Japan Industrial Bank.
Kodama fixed things. He was able to perform services
for cabinet officers, presidents of universities, presidents of coal mining companies and presidents of various industries all over Japan. You pile up a lot of *giri*
that way, and Mr. Kodama's method of collecting on the
debts owed him is to seek support for political candidates of his choosing. And he has managed to create a
base far greater than one which merely includes gangsters. As of today it is generally conceded that Kodama
is the vital contact point between the business community, the political community, the extremists in the reli-

gious community and the gangster community, and that he welcomes to his side any random groups of intellectuals and cultural jingoists who see eye-to-eye with him.

The *Yomiuri* reporter in his feature story tried pinning him down on those disavowals of extreme ultranationalism by mentioning the hefty contributions he has made to far-out superpatriotic groups, and Kodama smiled benignly. "Every now and then I run across youths who are thinking earnestly about the future of our country," he said, "denouncing not only the communists and socialists, but even the Liberal-Democratic Party as well. I am moved by their ardor—which is similar to that which I entertained when I was young—and I help them with money and in other ways from time to time."

Thanks to Kodama's introductions, Taoka began to gather strength in the Kanto area, and more and more men from the Yamaguchi-gumi began to show up in Yokohama and Tokyo and other previously taboo areas. There is no telling whether or not these actions might have resulted in a bloody all-out gang war with his most implacable and powerful foe, Inagawa, if a fortunate event (for Taoka) had not occurred. Inagawa himself was arrested, convicted and sentenced to a three-year term for operating a gambling game. That was in 1969, and without their strong man at the helm, the Inagawa gang became shaky. Affiliates began deserting, and police crackdowns all but decimated their ranks. They needed all their energy just to stay together, and had none left with which to oppose the Yamaguchi-gumi.

But it was no longer Taoka's strategy to simply march in and wipe up in the absence of his enemy. He had come a long way from sending men in ceremonial kimonos with swords and guns to rout out executives of the Meiyu-kai or the Honda-kai, to kill them as they knelt on their tatami mats. Instead he sent men in double-breasted suits with gifts to visit Inagawa in prison, to try to make his term as easy and pleasant as possible. Inagawa knew very well what had been happening to his gang, and he had seen the handwriting on the wall, so he appreciated these efforts on Taoka's part to make the inevitable more acceptable. On the day of his release, Yamaguchi-gumi men joined his own at the prison gates to honor him, and he was deeply touched that Taoka had enabled him to save face by making it seem that the merger had been one of choice, rather than something which had been forced upon him. It was all over but the brotherhood ceremony.

On an October morning in 1972, four black limousines drove down from Tokyo to the house in Kobe where I was to be received several months later, and ten men alighted from the cars. They were Inagawa's top executives, sent by Inagawa to work out the conditions for the alliance. For reasons best known to themselves, neither Taoka nor Inagawa was present.

As described in the *Mainichi Daily News* in a report on the merger, the representatives of both gangs sat cross-legged on the floor of the ceremonial room which I have mentioned—the one with the samurai armor in a glass case—facing one another over two *sambo* (small wooden tables for placing offerings to the gods). On each *sambo* was a sake cup, and a mediator intoned, "The ritual to tie the bond of brotherhood between

Kenichi Yamamoto, representing leader Taoka of the Yamaguchi-gumi, and Tadahiro Ishii, representing leader Inagawa of the Inagawa-kai, will now commence."

Sake was poured into the cups, and both men simultaneously drank, replaced the cups upside down and then picked them up again. They then placed them inside the folds of their kimonos at the breast, after which they firmly clasped each other's hands. The mediator then placed his hands over theirs and announced, "The sake cup of brotherhood ritual on even terms is over." A three-hour reception and meeting followed, and the war between the two giants was formally ended. For Taoka it was a dream fulfilled, for Inagawa it was hope for a new life, for the police it was one big headache.

Demonstrably, small neighborhood gangs warring among themselves were relatively easier to keep in check than the kind of behemoth Taoka had built. Now, with two such giants joined together, the task would seem impossible. As the Metropolitan Police Department of Tokyo has stated, "No longer will large-scale gang wars be possible because there is not a single gang, even in the traditionally gang-ridden Kanto area, strong enough to wage war with the combined forces of the Yamaguchi-Inagawa army."

Which does not mean that all other gangs will simply retire. There are still those which are extremely hostile to the Taoka invasion, and which are making their affiliations to build up strength, but as of now it would seem to be a fruitless adventure for any rival gangs to pit their strength against such a colossus. The Inagawa-kai currently controls a total of sixty-two underworld organi-

zations in seven prefectures, including Tokyo and Hokkaido. It is estimated that its monthly income totals
several tens of millions of yen. The Yamaguchi-gumi's
income is reputed to be ten times that amount at the
very least, and their sphere of influence was, before the
merger, almost all of Japan with the exception of those
covered by the Inagawa-kai. As a result of the merger,
only four prefectures in all of Japan are still independent of both, and nobody has much doubt that if the
Yamaguchi-Inagawa army should become interested,
the four would fall into their hands with little trouble.

A freelance reporter named Kenji Ino, who is an expert on *yakuza* activities, said of the new merger, "It can
be said that the structure of Japan's underworld organizations has taken a step nearer to that of the United
States . . . they have begun to reorganize along modern
lines, as a legitimate business." The sad tale which the
police recount is that some twenty-six thousand companies and shops in Japan are run by criminal gangs now,
their investments in these businesses having come from
smuggling, gambling, prostitution, drugs, loan shark-
ing, extortion, blackmail, the whole sorry list. The businesses themselves include bars, *pachinko* parlors, turkish baths, cabarets, construction companies, taxi
companies, factories and hotels. It is through these
fronts that the National Police Agency pins its hopes on
tracking down the big boys, and the number one target
is the *oyabun no oyabun,* Kazuo Taoka. In his case it is the
Koyo Forwarding Company which deals with freighting, longshoremen and harbor matters, and the Kobe
Geinosha which takes care of his entertainment enterprises that they are looking into. Taoka is outraged that
they are considered to be "fronts," or that they furnish

the bulk of Yamaguchi-gumi capital, and he is fighting the contention bitterly.

"That is simply a lie!" he states in his memoirs. "It's true that I am president of both companies, but they are absolutely independent of the Yamaguchi-gumi. In fact, the entire popular idea about the Yamaguchi-gumi is false. I cannot speak for other groups, but in my place people who like each other get together and share joy and sorrow. We are not engaged in business. All our members have outside jobs. Of course, if anything happens—a funeral, a wedding, some kind of ceremony—we all bring money to help. Some people have asked me some very impolite questions about rebates. I have too much pride to live with the assistance of my fellows. It is right and logical that seniors should take care of juniors, but we do it from our hearts, and we have no need of rebates."

It was the Metropolitan Police who referred to the Yamaguchi-Inagawa force as an "army." I don't know how literally they mean that, but I would imagine that this is the role which Yoshio Kodama envisages for them in the amalgamation of strange bedfellows which he has put together to replace the defunct Kanto-kai. It is called the Zen-ai-Kaigi, a short version of a lot of words which translate as the National Federation of Patriotic Organizations, and some people regard it as Kodama's masterpiece, although true to his vow to remain *kuromaku*, he merely sits on the board instead of leading the organization. He has no desire to hog the spotlight. In that position there is an infinitely more dramatic figure, the current president whose name is Keizo Takei.

Keizo Takei is no run-of-the-mill patriot. He is, if you please, a religious leader with full status as a Buddhist grand monk, and he sees nothing strange in his alliance with gangsters in the name of patriotism. "For the survival of our country," he has said, "we would do anything—even kill. We have already used force and won. What would a monk be if he did not love his country?" I suppose he could be a monk who loves his country well enough to want to rid it of its antisocial elements like gangsters, for one thing.

Kodama's choice of Takei to lead the parade of rightists which he has brought together is an inspiration which a fiction writer would eschew as being too whimsical. A Buddhist monk clad in white robes presiding over uniformed *yakuza*? Too melodramatic. The passionate patriot is in his early sixties, about the same age as both Kodama and Taoka. He is totally bald, round-faced and powerfully built, his eyes burn with the fever of a zealot and his jaw is set in grim determination as he speaks of the danger to his country from the press, which he sees as dominated by the left, and from certain elements in the government which he scorns for not putting the best interests of Japan ahead of their desire to become part of the world community.

His monkish facade has not prevented Takei from piling up impeccable credentials as a radical activist. He owns and operates a thirty-man task force who go where he tells them and does what he orders. One of their steadier jobs in the past was guarding the safety of the former prime minister, Eisaku Sato, who was approved of by the *yakuza* and other rightists, and who had had Kodama's blessing. This security force was withdrawn when the subsequent prime minister, Tanaka, was elected. Kodama had worked against Tanaka, who was not, apparently, part of his "in" group. In all fairness, it should be noted that Eisaku Sato had not requested this bodyguard service from his admiring friends, and when asked why he had supplied it, according to a journalist who did a story for the *Mainichi Daily News* on the Zen-ai-Kaigi, Takei shrugged his shoulders and replied, "What is wrong with a man 'falling in love' with another man and serving him as a bodyguard?" The same story quotes a gangster leader who was asked about the curious relationships which exist between the monk, gangsters, politicians and business leaders, and said, "We are bound by the same belief and principles."

Takei is very proud of the power he is able to muster when the occasion demands it. For example, on the occasion of Eisenhower's visit to Japan, Kodama had been approached *by the police* to do something about the left-wing demonstration which was expected against Eisenhower, so he put the matter into Takei's able hands and the result was eighteen thousand *yakuza* lining the way from Haneda airport all the way to the Emperor's Palace, interspersed by a like number of cops at strategic points.

But not all of Takei's activities have been on such an officially sanctioned level. He admits to having been involved in a few extortion cases, has been arrested no less than forty times and has spent three weeks in police custody. His face relaxes into an unaccustomed smile when he adds, in relating this story, that several of the policemen who arrested him were demoted to lower ranks. The Takeis of Japan have no fear of the hard-working and frustrated police. Their protection obviously comes from more powerful bodies.

In addition to Takei, another religious leader sits on the board of Zen-ai-Kaigi, this one a Christian pastor named Bokusii Arihara. His "peace movement" during the war landed him in jail for a while, and he had been involved with a group who attempted to assassinate a prime minister during the '30s, and had lately been party to an extortion case affecting a major construction company. All of this, of course, does not cancel out the fact that he too is a burning patriot. And not on the board but members in good standing are people like Inagawa, Taoka's new comrade-in-arms, who explains virtuously, "We gamblers are considered outlaws by the society, but if we unite and try to prevent communism from invading the country, we can do a great service." And another gangster member says, "It is just that we wish to have a voice in politics, as do socialistic organizations and labor unions. We wish to become useful to the country." The thought has crossed the minds of police and other cynics that they could accomplish this noble purpose by simply going out of business.

There is nothing secret about the Zen-ai-Kaigi. It has attracted lunatic fringe groups of rightist radicals, reminiscent of the private army trained and led by the late Yukio Mishima who saw themselves as Japan's only hope for defense against the decadence of the Western influence. But it also attracts rather more solid citizens from the business and political communities. And of course, gangsters. The *Mainichi* story told how two hundred fifty of these people met solemnly in the summer of '73 in a hall of a Buddhist temple in Chiba prefecture. The two hundred fifty were delegates from their various organizations, the bulk of them being young men with close-cropped haircuts, wearing their *yakuza* gang emblems on khaki or blue uniforms. (To me, at least, it conjures up a picture of a beer hall in Munich, where the rallying cry was also anti-communism. I am still gun-shy from the result of that meeting, so perhaps I am overreacting, but dedicated fanatics are certainly capable of creating havoc in times of stress.) There was also an invitee from the Liberal-Democratic Party representing a "study group" led by a former prime minister.

The first speaker was an affluent *oyabun* who walked out of his white Lincoln Continental and into the hall, guarded by two of his *kobun*. "I am a *yakuza* and I am proud of it," was his opening statement, "but what could be more deplorable than the fact that a *yakuza* is invariably mistaken for a gangster?" The speaker was a man named Yamada, and in addition to being a *yakuza*, he is president of a tile company, a building company, an entertainment company and a few other corporations, all of which are based in Osaka, firmly Yamaguchi-gumi territory. He followed his opening remarks with an attack on international communist banditry, on the biased educational system controlled by the left-wing teachers' organization which brainwashes children with "liberal" nonsense, and of course, ended his speech with suitable expressions of loyalty to the Emperor.

He was followed by a Tokyo *oyabun* who also stated his affiliation, voiced the same sentiments as his predecessor and added, "The mass media, being infiltrated

by communists, says we are a violent antisocial element.
The truth is that we are peace-loving and always on the
side of the weak. We live in the tradition of Japan." The
LDP member explained his presence by saying, "We
are committed to one objective. Mr. Sato (the former
prime minister) has said that what we need today is a
spiritual restoration. I volunteered to attend this meeting because we share the same view that we must
uphold our national dignity and identity." But the
speech which seemed best to pinpoint the purpose of
the meeting was made by a vice president of the federation in which he said, "When we decide that a crisis is
close by, we will resign from 'all official posts' to be free
to take our own action. We have our own private organizations which we can commit to save the nation from
a communist takeover. Our resolution is that we are
ready to offer our lives for the sake of the nation, but
not before each of us takes fifty enemy lives."

The Zen-ai-Kaigi controls some five hundred gangster-rightist organizations with a total estimated membership of one hundred fifty thousand, and it is not the
only such federation. An even more radical group
which is a spin-off of the Zen-ai-Kaigi is called the Seishi-kai, which stands for Youth Group for the Study of
Ideologies. It too has gangster leaders on its board,
plus the president of Oshu University and other respectable community leaders. Among the gangster
leaders is the Korean *oyabun* Chong Kyu Young, who
had been so helpful to Taoka in bringing him into the
Kanto area. (The Tosei-kai, which he led, he is alleged
to have disbanded, and he has also given up his Korean
name, since it is easier to function in Japan with a Japanese name. He is now known as Hisayuki Machii, and

is a most successful businessman, chiefly in the entertainment field and in several joint Japanese-Korean
economic ventures.) The Seishi-kai is also under the
benevolent eye of Yoshio Kodama.

According to the *Daily Mainichi,* some three hundred
thousand are involved in gangster-rightist organizations, and approximately two million people are identified with one or another student, religious, cultural
and political organization of strongly right-wing colora-
tion. Small wonder that the monk Takei boasts that he
could organize a coup d'etat in a day. "I have the
money," he says, "and I have the men."

The radical left in Japan boasts no such affluence or
extensive organization as does the radical right—nevertheless it has shown itself capable of creating grave
disorder and extensive violence. The rioting in the
streets by student activists in the '60s, the fire bomb-
ings, the close-down of universities—all these were
manifestations of the far left, as they were in France and
certainly in our own country. More recently the Japanese New Left, the "red guard" so to speak, has made
common cause with Arab terrorists, the most notorious
of their violent adventures having been the murder of
hapless travelers in an Israeli airport. It is such activities
which the ultrarightists can point to in order to give
legitimacy to their own organization as a counterforce,
but in fact it is not against these extremists that their fire
is directed, but against the more liberal elements in
their government, against the press, and in fact against
any progressive forces in the country who would reject
extreme conservatism as a way of life.

My learned friend the historian, to whom I had expressed fears about the Zen-ai-Kaigi and other such

organizations, shrugged and said, "They're getting along in years—Kodama, Takei and company. They're brilliant and wily planners, it's true, and nobody underestimates their clout when it comes to influencing legislation and acting as a lobby, but actually they're not in the mainstream of Japanese thinking. We're basically a conservative people, you know, and the overwhelming majority of us would reject any attempt to lead us back to feudalism or any militant effort on the part of the left to take us over. We had our bellyful of extremism before World War II."

"And you don't think they're to be feared?" I asked.

"I didn't say that, did I?" he replied. "A really tough depression could probably give their movement a lot of impetus, but we're watching them, never fear."

All of which makes me pray for continued prosperity in Japan. A serious setback in their economy would almost certainly give both the extreme left and the extreme right momentum for an armed confrontation. My historian friend may not be afraid, but the thought of a hundred fifty thousand armed *yakuza* united in a cause is pretty scary to me. And "mainstreams of thought" have been known to change their course.

CHAPTER 13

I HAVEN'T meant to give the impression that the rank-and-file *yakuza* is a political theoretician. The chances are that the strong-arm boys ringing the Buddhist shrine where the Zen-ai-Kaigi holds its conclaves are bored with all the political palaver and would much prefer to be playing *hana-fuda* somewhere, but they are good soldiers, committed to the group ethic, who will most certainly follow the policy laid down for them by their *oyabun*.

The brains at the top may be interested in politics, but the rank-and-file men don't really care, and besides, man cannot live by politics alone—not if he's a *yakuza*.

Unless he is in the strategy-planning inner circle, he's stuck with the bread-and-butter chores: twisting the arm of storekeepers and cafe owners for a percentage of the take, pimping, hustling suckers into gambling games, being a dealer, a bartender, a bodyguard, an enforcer, whatever his specialty may be, peddling drugs and porno movies, looking after mah-jongh parlors and turkish baths, smuggling and the rest. It might not be as lofty as the higher purpose which people like Kodama have in mind for him, but it's a living.

Nor is it any bed of roses. There's always the possibility of getting a knife or a sword driven through your innards, or of being shot in the newer *gurentai* way, or of being maimed in a number of rather unpleasant ways, or of having to live like a rat, hiding out in holes from your rivals or from the harassment of the police. Harassment is about the best one can say for the efforts of the law-enforcement bodies, even though one does continually read of the roundup of thousands of gangsters. If past history is any gauge, most of them will be freed or get off with light sentences, and those who go to jail will come out and find that their place has been kept open for them in their absence, and they may even get a nice present from the *oyabun*. As long as there is a market for their public services, they are not going out of business.

And supposing by some remote chance all these thousands had a mass conversion to the straight and narrow, there are plenty more where they came from. There are the young delinquents (the ones called *chimpira*), frustrated *burakumin,* some emotional basketcases and others tired of unrelieved poverty, all warming up in the wings, hoping to be recruited. There are recruiting officers in the gangs looking for such people, "youth captains" they are called, ready and able to train them in the life of the *yakuza*. (Not the sons of the bosses, it would appear. Taoka didn't send his son Mitsuru to Keio University to make a *yakuza* of him, and the *oyabun* who spoke with Bernie Krisher told him that he would have retired long ago except for the fact that he wants to keep the younger *yakuza* in line, and also to make sure that none of his own sons were tempted to join up. Neither of them is ashamed of the life he has led, but both want something better for their own children—something which they bought for them with blood.)

With the merger of the Yamaguchi-gumi with the Inagawa-kai, it would seem that the covered-wagon days for Taoka are finished, that he might well settle back in his house in Kobe and relax, but actually there are still jobs to be done. For one thing, big as they are, the Yamaguchi-gumi must constantly remain alert against plotters in small gangs who, while they do not dare to challenge them now, could be biding their time and making allies. For another thing, there are still frontiers. The newly reverted Okinawa, for example, where already Yamaguchi-gumi advance guards have been seen, to the dismay of the police and the local big-shot gang leaders who are prepared to fight them with bazookas, if necessary. (They have the bazookas, as it happens, courtesy of the U.S. occupying soldiers, who were glad to sell them to the locals.) And I am told there are negotiations afoot with gangs in other countries for international cooperation. I can't vouch for it, but it sounds plausible. Another frontier is that of regional politics, with attempts being made to infiltrate gang members into local municipal assemblies. That's comparatively small, but it's a new direction and worth noting.

Yes, in the autumn of his life, Taoka can certainly count himself a success, and so far he is still a free man. If he requires proof of his eminence, he has imitators trying to cash in on his name. In spring 1974 a small group of hoodlums tried prying protection money out of people in Tokyo, Chiba, and Saitama prefectures by using the name of the Yamaguchi-gumi. The gangsters visited a construction site, routed out the contractor, and after presenting name cards which said "Yamaguchi-gumi Shinanokai Kanto Branch," they said, "Our group is taking over this neighborhood." They approached about one hundred people and extracted some four million yen before they were caught up with and it was proved that they had no connection whatever with the Yamaguchi-gumi.

Even the wedding of his son Mitsuru to a beautiful young actress named Hideko Nakamura in the spring of 1974 was more a public occasion for paying tribute to Kazuo Taoka than a celebration of a wedding. A friend sent me a clipping out of a paper called *Tokyo Total,* in which an account by a *yakuza*-watcher named Andrew Horvat was contained. Mr. Horvat listed as wedding guests many of the people I have mentioned. Notably present was Seigen Tanaka, the right-wing political strong man who had been so helpful to Taoka. And there was a scattering of people in the arts, including Ken Takakura and Koji Tsuruta, the famous *yakuza* actors, mixing it up with their real-life counterparts, lapping up the Johnnie Walker Black Label (which I just happen to remember from my own stay there was going for twenty-eight dollars a bottle) in toasts to the happy couple. There was also the former mayor of Kobe, a Liberal-Democratic Party member of the Diet, Noboru Goto who heads the Tokyo Railroad and a string of plush hotels, the head of Mitsubishi Warehouses, the head of Tokuma Publishing Company, Shigeru Okada who is chief of the Toei Motion Picture Company, and a whole string of other wheels in the non-*yakuza* world. Telegrams of felicitation were sent by Nobosuke Kishi, former prime minister of Japan; Eitaro Itoyama, an LDP candidate for the Upper House; and Ryoichi Sasagawa, who is almost an equal to Yoshio Kodama in the rightist world. As there were seven hundred invited guests, they were not all listed, but Mr. Horvat noted that there were one hundred fifty representatives from Taoka's affiliated organizations.

Kazuo Taoka was unquestionably the star of the occasion, for most of the speeches had not to do so much with Mitsuru-san and Hideko-san, but were instead proclamations of Taoka's greatness. Seigen Tanaka spoke (for forty minutes) of the time when he and the elder Taoka had "rid the Japanese underworld of hard drugs" (obviously not a permanent state of affairs considering that they are now the greatest source of revenue for the underworld), and another speech by a dignitary thanked Taoka for "helping to maintain law and order during those perilous postwar years."

Mr. Horvat ends his account with this: "Of course, no one should suggest that the presence of all these famous and powerful people in any way meant that they either approved or condoned the methods of the hoods with whom they shared the wedding feast.

"No. For after all, they are honorable men."

It's a long way from being a scruffy hooligan sleeping on a tatami mat in a *gonzo-heya* to being the toast of industrialists, members of the Diet and former prime ministers. All told, it took Kazuo Taoka a quarter of a century to fulfill his promise to his *kobun*—"Just as Japan will be reborn, the Yamaguchi-gumi will be reborn"—and to change the entire structure of the *yakuza* world from a lot of neighborhood gangs into a huge conglomerate, an unparalleled success in the history of gangsterism in Japan.

In spite of the testimonials, nobody is presenting Taoka with a gold watch in expectation of his retirement, although the police keep hoping. As far back as 1965, the dossier which had been compiled on the Yamaguchi-gumi and Kazuo Taoka contained what looked like an obituary: "If we view him as the architect of the Yamaguchi-gumi in the structure of our social history, he *was* quite a man. There has never existed a *yakuza* group which shed so much blood and disturbed the social order, stored illegal assets, maintained so strong an organization and such firm unity as the Yamaguchi-gumi. Taoka, as the head of this organization, did this all with his own personal will and power, and with all his misdeeds and crimes, has never been imprisoned since he attained his place as the third *oya-bun* of the Yamaguchi-gumi." If, in speaking of him in the past tense, there was ever a piece of wishful thinking, that was it. They really felt they had put an end to the Yamaguchi-gumi because various of the front organizations were declaring themselves independent of the gang. The only sticker was that they were doing it with Taoka's approval—his urging, in fact—as part of his plan for legitimacy. It made no practical difference to the workings and the income of the gang, since they were all still under orders from the boss.

The police were certainly right about the "firm unity." They had commented in another part of that report that Taoka has a genius for picking the right man for the right job, men whose skill and ruthlessness in the execution of their duties are matched by their loyalty to the boss. That's quite a knack, especially when you consider that the new look among gangsters these days, since the entry of the *gurentai* on the scene, is one of relationships based more on expedience than on mutual obligation and duty. And yet, Kazuo Taoka continues to evoke almost legendary loyalty from his *kobun*, although he commands the biggest conglomerate of them all.

There is however the undeniable fact that, like me, Taoka isn't as young as he once was. There's that heart condition, the trembling hands, the pallor, the inevitable physical slow-down. It hasn't affected his brain, and I doubt that there's a single Yamaguchi-gumi member who wants him to step down while he is still capable of directing the affairs of the organization, which he would appear to be. They want him as the godfather of godfathers until they carry him out. Which is not to say that there isn't a little in-fighting about who will succeed him. Without Taoka's inspired leadership, there are many who feel that the organization will come unglued at his death, and the police can hardly be blamed for looking forward to that eventuality. My guess is that the hard core of Yamaguchi-gumi leaders are at the draw-ing board with plans to keep the firm intact. It is be-lieved that Yamamoto, the man who stood in for Taoka at the brotherhood ceremony with the Inagawa-kai, is the heir apparent, but it is also possible that with tradi-tions going by the boards so quickly, it will be run more on a board-of-directors basis than on the indispens-able-man principle. The board of directors will have to work very hard to match Taoka's talent as a master tactician and a public-relations man. He has created a personality cult, and the *yakuza* world will be a poorer and less interesting place without him. Not that it won't go on. Just as long as there is a market for their pro-ducts, and just as long as there are those elements in society which have their uses for gangsters and which are powerful enough to protect them, they'll be around.

As of now, however, Kazuo Taoka is very much alive, and unless the police really do nail him for taxes, he's going to sit right there in that house in Kobe being the gray eminence of the *yakuza* world. As he said when the police once tried to pressure him into quitting, "Cer-tainly, I'll be glad to do it provided the country will provide us with ten thousand dollars per member to help them in their rebirth!"

That could be a bargain price to pay if he really meant it, but he doesn't. I have that on the authority of some-one who knows him perhaps better than he knows him-self, his wife. The newspaper of the Yamaguchi-gumi, the *Jiho*, carries along with its other features a "Letters to the Editor" column. In an issue in 1973 there was a letter from the beloved *Anesan*, Fumiko Taoka. As I read it, I could see her bustling around the living room, carrying trays of delicacies for her husband and son and Mr. Chang and the strange American lady. I remember wondering what she was thinking. I know now, for in her rueful little note she said that she wished her husband would give up his life of crime, "if only for the sake of the children," but, she added, she realized the impossibility of persuading him to do that because he "looks too happy when he talks about the events of the day."

EPILOGUE

CONSTANT outward change seems to be the pattern of Japan. It is not easy to wallow in nostalgia when one returns to this endlessly fascinating country, to revisit remembered pastoral places tucked away in the corner of a heart, for they will likely have disappeared, their calm and peace displaced by industrial complexes. There is probably no country in the world where change is more blatantly visible, more dramatic and dynamic than in Japan. How could it be otherwise, when one considers the staggering fact that in the space of a quarter of a century it has gone from a bombed-out, defeated nation to one of the great powers of the world? And since all this was accomplished not through luck, and certainly not through endowment of great natural resources, one can only be filled with enormous admiration for the herculean efforts of a remarkable people who made it all happen.

To a foreigner, it seems that the people who have brought about these phenomenal changes have also been transformed. Their clothes are different, their manner more relaxed; they seem not to be steeped so deeply in tradition, to have become thoroughly modern from the Western point of view. Madame Butterfly is an anachronism. There is no time for languishing in the bustling twentieth century scene of modern Japan, where everyone appears to have accepted a new view of life.

Appears, however, is the operative word, for I would venture the opinion that there is less internal change than there is external accommodation to fit the new facts of life in Japan. No longer agrarian, no longer militaristic, Japan is an industrial nation, and her people look and behave like the people of other industrial nations, but I submit that the changes about which so much has been written are more visible than real. It is true that some old concepts and traditions have been put aside, or at least altered and molded to fit the times, as a hem on a dress might be lowered or raised, but the basic fashion remains the same. The factors which characterize Japanese society have not been uprooted to any noticeable degree.

The most persistent of these factors is that Japan is now, as it always has been, a hierarchical society. The informal structure through which it functions is a system of groups, in which every member has a well-defined place, each group being headed by a ruling figure who keeps his position of authority just as long as he is able to maintain harmony within the group. It is a system with which the vast majority of the Japanese people are most comfortable, for while it does not allow for much flexibility or upward mobility among the members of the group, it furnishes something more important to the Japanese, a stable place in society, and a great deal of security. What has not changed in Japan is the concept that it is better to fit in than to stand out, and the most admired leaders of society are not the brilliant individualists with radical concepts for change, but those who are committed to the idea of consensus, even if the consensus is wrong. The pace of Japan has quickened, but for all its new, modern Western clothes, it still marches to the rhythm of what has been called "the kimono heart."

In exact step with that rhythm are the *yakuza*. Vigorous adherents to the group system, their hierarchy differs from the rest of the country only in that it clings even more tenaciously to tradition—so much so that the *yakuza* seem sometimes to be the ones who are truly the upholders of old values and national identity. They have less need than their compatriots to give up old customs, since they are not dependent upon international approval or connections for their livelihood—but with that exception, they are indistinguishable from the rest of society in the way they function as an organization. It is that which makes it so difficult for outsiders to detect them, and for the forces of law and order within the country to uproot them. The fact that they proclaim themselves openly to be *yakuza* at political get-togethers of the far right, or on other public occa-

sions which celebrate somebody coming out of jail or
the installation of a new *oyabun* in a gang, does not give
the police *carte blanche* to step in and round them up.
Such action would be possible in a totalitarian state, but
Japan has a democratic constitution modeled after our
own, and is committed as we are to protection of the
civil rights of all her citizens, good and bad. There are,
of course, roundups of criminals, but they are based on
specific criminal activities. It is no crime to announce
one's affiliation with an organization which claims to be
a "self-help and friendship group." Everyone may sus-
pect or even know differently, but as with us, it takes
more than suspicion to obtain convictions in court.

Nor is it a crime to join in with the superpatriots of
the radical right. As of now, ultranationalism is not in
the mainstream of Japanese thinking, but neither is it
against the law. They have every right to rail against the
"decadence" of government, press, education and
youth, to issue broadsides and to try to influence public
opinion, so long as they commit no overt acts of violence. From their point of view, they stand in defense
of true Japanese values, as opposed to the alien philosophy of the radical left.

The *yakuza*, in every phase of their centuries-long
history, have gone to great lengths to court public opinion, to make themselves palatable. Feudal Robin
Hoods, champions of the oppressed, postwar defenders of the national honor, and their current posture of
patriotism and of wishing to maintain the system exactly as it is are the romantic cloaks which sometimes
obscure the true nature of their criminal activities from
even decent, honest citizens. The fact is that only an
aroused and united citizenry could actually succeed in

ridding the country of *yakuza*, and that's not easy. Not as long as there are powerful elements of the society which find them useful.

But the remarkable degree of tolerance for the *yakuza* extends to many who are not powerful or superpatriotic, and it struck me that this was because, despite the numbers of Koreans and Chinese within their ranks, they are essentially a Japanese institution. It is impossible to overstate the degree to which the Japanese feel their national identity—more than in any country I have ever visited—and the *yakuza*, unloved by most, are nevertheless "us," as Mr. Nakahira of the National Police Agency put it. They are not some strange, foreign group which has imposed itself on the culture as did the mafia in our country, nor did they appear suddenly like a plague. Having been around for centuries, they are more like a chronic disease, something to be borne— a pain which is alleviated when it becomes too acute, by purges and arrests, but otherwise sighed over and regretted as an uncomfortable part of one's self.

Maintaining a low profile for the most part throughout the years, the *yakuza* have worked very hard at not becoming too painful to be borne. Their capacity to bend with the wind and to gauge the degree of tolerance toward them has worked for them. Where the pressures of society have forced them to retreat, they have retreated, coming out into the open again when the pressure has abated. Where police crackdowns have closed some avenues of revenue, or at least decreased their activities, society has furnished them with some new ones—sometimes unwittingly, sometimes with cynical knowledge. They are the paid bully-boys of labor conflicts, and they are the *sokaiya* who are hired by big business and who then blackmail their employers. As a release for their aggressions, the ultranationalists of the political arena have furnished them with a paramilitarist front, potentially capable of conflict and violence far beyond any inner gang struggles. And with their talent for blending into the scenery, the *yakuza* have learned the pattern for survival in the twentieth century, by remodeling the little neighborhood gangs into vast cartels with outside investments, and with respectable fronts to mask their activities.

To predict what the *yakuza* of the future will look like, one would have to be able to predict what the Japan of the future will look like, for they will take their cue from that, marching in the same direction as their fellow citizens, as inconspicuously as possible. That they will totally disappear seems highly unlikely, and whatever they seem to be externally, they will cling to the same rituals, traditions and codes which have been the glue that has bound them together for centuries as a unified force. As in the rest of the country, the changes are more apparent than real, and it makes no difference whether they wear kimonos, brown shirts or double-breasted suits. Underneath are the tattoos which brand them for what they are.

GLOSSARY

ANDO, NOBORU A former *yakuza*, once convicted of murder, currently an actor and singer.

Anesan Literally "older sister," but used in the *yakuza* world as a term of respect for the boss's wife.

ARIHARA, BOKUSII An officer of the Zen-ai-Kaigi, who happens also to be a Christian pastor, and who has a prison record because of his involvement in illegal activities.

Bakuto *Yakuza* whose specialty is gambling. Formerly this was their only activity, but they have branched out into other fields.

BONNO Real name MASAO SUGAYA, also known as NAKAGASHIRA. Early ally of Kazuo Taoka in the period after World War II. Nicknamed "Rascal."

Boryokudan Violence gangs. This is the term by which the police prefer the gangs should be known, rather than *yakuza*.

Buraku Ghettos, the traditional dwelling places of the descendants of the *eta* class of feudal Japan.

Burakumin Those who live in *buraku*.

Bushi The samurai, the military aristocracy.

Bushido "The way of the warrior"; the code by which the samurai were supposed to have lived, embracing stoic endurance, scorn of danger or death, religious worship of sovereign and country.

CHANG, S. Tokyo correspondent, *Time* magazine.

Chimpira Juvenile delinquents, young hoods who are a recruiting pool for *yakuza*.

CHOBEI, BANZUIIN Seventeenth-century *yakuza* hero in the Robin Hood tradition, first known *oyabun* of gamblers, labor recruiter, ex-samurai.

Dani Literally "parasitic worm," figuratively a pimp.

Dewa matta So long, see you later.

EDO   Formerly the name of Tokyo. The Edo period embraces the time beginning in 1603, when the shogun Tokugawa selected Edo as his residence and built a castle there which remained the seat of the shogunate until 1868. The name of Edo was changed to Tokyo that year, and the following year the Meiji Restoration saw it become the seat of government and the residence of the emperor.

Eta   A class of laborers of feudal Japan, equivalent to that of the Indian untouchables, who performed defiling labors. The class is now outlawed as such, but the memory lingers on. Civil rights organizations are at work on their behalf, but the social stigma persists.

FUKAYAMA, FUMIKO   Maiden name of Mrs. Taoka.

FURUKAWA, "BIG EYES"   Right-hand man of Noboru Yamaguchi, and mentor under whose guidance Kazuo Taoka served his apprenticeship in the Yamaguchi-gumi.

Gaijin   A foreigner.

Giri   Duty, based on obligation, a debt of gratitude.

Gonzo-heya   A barracks-like accommodation for itinerant laborers, construction workers, waterfront longshoremen and the like.

GREENFIELD, JAMES   Foreign editor, *New York Times.*

H., MR.   A *yakuza* boss, controls a nightclub area and is involved in show business.

Hai   Yes.

Hajiki   *Yakuza* slang for a "heater," gun.

Hajimemashite   Literally "first time." Proper reply to acknowledge an introduction.

Hakama   Loose Japanese trousers, which resemble a pleated skirt.

Hana-fuda   Flower cards, used in gambling.

Hana-kogyo   Flower show, which has nothing to do with flowers. It is a theatrical presentation, featuring a single star. *Hana* is the word for flower or for nose, depending on accent and context.

Haori   Japanese coat, about knee-length.

Happi-coat   A short, about hip-length kimono.

HASEGAWA, KAZUO   Actor, ex-Toei star, ran afoul of *yakuza.*

Himo   Literally "string," *yakuza* slang for a pimp.

HIRATA   *Oyabun,* Hirata-kai, affiliate of Honda-kai, former rival of Yamaguchi-gumi. Extreme rightist.

HONDA, JINSUKE   *Oyabun,* Honda-kai. Organized gamblers into second-biggest gang in Taoka's territory. Eventually routed by Yamaguchi-gumi.

IKEDA, DAISAKU   Spiritual leader of Soka Gakkai.

INAGAWA, KAKUJI   Powerful *oyabun,* Inagawa-kai, involved in rightist politics, the big boss of the Kanto area. Currently associated with Taoka.

Ippiki-okami   A lone wolf. In Japan, a pejorative term.

ISHII, ICHIRO   *Oyabun,* Ishii-gumi, affiliated with the Yamaguchi-gumi.

Jingi   A code of justice and humanity, formerly a samurai word, now used almost exclusively by *yakuza.*

Kakko-yosa   A *yakuza* term meaning "one of the gang."

Kamikaze   Literally "The Great Wind." Used to describe a suicide mission.

KAMODA   *Oyabun,* Kamoda-gumi, affiliate of the Yamaguchi-gumi.

Kampai!   Cheers! Down the hatch!

KANSAI   Western Japan.

KANTO   Eastern Japan.

Katagi   Honest people, the straight world.

Katana   A short sword.

KAWADA, HARUHISA   *Rokyoku* singer, helped Taoka get started in show business.

KISHI, N.   Former prime minister.

KOBE GEINOSHA A theatrical agency controlling performers, theaters, etc., of which K. Taoka was the founder and president.

Kobun Literally "child role." The members of the gang.

KODAMA, YOSHIO The most powerful rightist leader in Japan, referred to in the press as the *oyabun* of the right.

Konketsu Mixed blood.

KOYO FORWARDING COMPANY An agency dealing with waterfront business, of which K. Taoka was the founder and president.

KRISHER, BERNARD Tokyo bureau chief, *Newsweek* magazine.

KUROYANAGI, TETSUKO Actress, writer, TV personality.

Machi-yakko Literally "town guards." Early *yakuza*, lower echelon samurai.

MEIYU-KAI A conglomerate of Korean gangsters, formerly operating in Taoka's territory. Routed by Yamaguchi-gumi.

MISHIMA, YUKIO Author, playwright, actor, Nobel candidate, fervent nationalist who committed suicide to dramatize Japan's "capitulation" to Western "decadence."

MISORA, HIBARI Leading popular singer in Japan, protégée of K. Taoka, client of M. Taoka.

MIYAZAWA, ARTHUR Businessman, historian, teacher.

Mizushobai Literally "water business." Slang for certain night-life restaurants and cafes.

NAKAHIRA, Mr. Chief, Second Section, National Police Agency, charged with *yakuza* activities.

Nawabari Territory.

Nawabari-arasoi Territorial disputes.

Ninjo Obligation based on humanity, as opposed to *giri.*

ODA, JOJI Former *kobun* who acted as secretary to Taoka.

Resigned or fired for dereliction of duty; started own gang, Oda-gumi, with help of *tekiya.* Remains affiliated with Yamaguchi-gumi.

Oreimairi To give thanks. In *yakuza* slang, to destroy the premises of anyone who refuses "protection."

Oyabun Literally "father role." The boss of the gang, among *yakuza.* The dominant male figure in other areas of life.

Pachinko A pinball-game machine.

Rokyoku A form of folk singing, combining heroic tales.

Sambo Low ceremonial tables, for offerings.

Samurai A noble class of warriors, guards; the only class permitted the use of swords. Pre-Restoration.

San Mr., Mrs., Miss.

Sangokujin Third Country people; Korean and Chinese residents of Japan.

Sanshita Apprentice.

SASAKI, MICHIO *Oyabun,* Sasaki-gumi, inner council of Yamaguchi-gumi.

SATO, EISAKU Former prime minister.

Seishi-kai An ultranationalist organization.

Shinde moraimasu! I will have your life! A *yakuza* confrontation expression.

Shinrai dekimasu Reliable, trustworthy.

Shogun The chief military officer in pre-Meiji Restoration Japan, virtually the ruler of the country although his title was always conferred by the emperor.

Soka Gakkai The Nichiren Shoshu sect of Buddhism, claims ten million members in Japan and other countries, including the United States. Politically conservative, it is the spiritual arm of the Komeito, third-largest party in Japan.

Sokaiya "General-meeting experts," a new wrinkle in *yakuza* activities, used for intimidating stockholders.

STRICKLAND, ROBERT Businessman, restaurateur, one-time entertainer, long-time resident of Japan.

Suke *Yakuza* slang for girls, gangsters' girls, that is.

TAKAKURA, KEN Leading actor of Japan in *yakuza* roles.

TAMIYA, JIRO Star of stage and screen, sometimes plays *yakuza* roles.

TANAKA, KAKUEI Prime minister of Japan.

TANAKA, SEIGEN Rightist boss, friend of Taoka.

TAOKA, KAZUO *Oyabun no oyabun,* godfather of godfathers.

TAOKA, MITSURU Kazuo's son, a theatrical agent and movie producer.

Tekiya Specialty *yakuza,* formerly only street-stall operators, currently branching out.

TSUKUDA, RYOICHI Former member of the Diet, present at the installation of Taoka as *oyabun* of the Yamaguchi-gumi.

TSURUTA, KOJI Actor in *yakuza* roles, friend of Taoka.

Yagura A miniature tower trophy in sumo wrestling.

Yakuza A gangster, gangsters.

Yakuza-eiga The gangster-film genre.

YAMADA, "TIGER" Pal of Taoka's young *yakuza* days, companion in mayhem.

YAMAMOTO, FUJIKO An actress who ran afoul of the *yakuza* and became unemployable.

YAMAMOTO, Y. Taoka lieutenant in Yamaguchi-gumi, rumored to be first in line as his successor.

YANAGIGAWA Also called YANG. Korean *oyabun* of a gang which is affiliated with Yamaguchi-gumi.

YOSAKURA, GINJI Colorful, defunct member of Yamaguchi-gumi whose death resulted in their takeover of another territory.

YOUNG, CHONG KYU Also called HISAYUKI MACHII.

Oyabun of the Tosei-kai, leading Korean mob in the Kanto area; Taoka's connection.

Zen-ai-Kaigi Amalgamation of gangster and rightist organizations, brain child of Yoshio Kodama.

BIBLIOGRAPHY

ALLEN, G. C., *A Short Economic History of Modern Japan*, G. Allen & Unwin, London, 1946.

AXELBANK, A., *Black Star over Japan*, Charles E. Tuttle, Tokyo, 1973.

BENEDICT, RUTH, *The Chrysanthemum and the Sword*, Charles E. Tuttle, Tokyo, 1946.

COLE, ROBERT E., *Japanese Blue Collar*, University of California Press, Berkeley, 1971.

DEVOS AND MIZUSHIMA, *Aspects of Social Change in Modern Japan*, ed. R. P. Dore, Princeton University Press, Princeton, 1971.

DEVOS AND WAGATSUMA, *Japan's Invisible Race*, University of California Press, Berkeley, 1966.

DOI, DR. TAKEO, *The Anatomy of Dependence*, Kodansha International, Tokyo, 1973.

FUJIWARA, DR. HIROTATSU, *I Denounce Soka Gakkai*, trans. W. C. Grant, Nisshin Hoda Co., Tokyo, 1970.

GIBNEY, FRANK, *Five Gentlemen of Japan*, Charles E. Tuttle, Tokyo, 1953, 1973.

HALL, JOHN WHITNEY, *Japan from Prehistory to Modern Times*, Charles E. Tuttle, Tokyo, 1971.

HALLORAN, RICHARD, *Japan, Images and Realities*, Charles E. Tuttle, Tokyo, 1970.

IKEDA, DAISAKU, *The Human Revolution*, Weatherhill, Tokyo, 1972.

KAHN, HERMAN, *Emerging Japanese Superstate: Challenge and Response*, Prentice Hall, Englewood Cliffs, N.J., 1970.

KATA, KOJI, *Japanese Yakuza*, Daiwa Shobo, Tokyo, 1964.

KENNEDY, MALCOLM, *A Short History of Japan*, Charles E. Tuttle, Tokyo, 1963.

MINISTRY OF FOREIGN AFFAIRS, *Japan in Transition*, International Society for Educational Information, Tokyo, 1972.

NAKANE, CHIE, *Japanese Society*, University of California Press, Berkeley, 1972.

NITOBE, INAZO, *Bushido, the Soul of Japan*, Charles E. Tuttle, Tokyo, 1969.

SEWARD, J., *The Japanese*, Lotus Press, Tokyo, 1971.

TADASU, IZAWA, *Outline of Tattooing Art.*

TAOKA, KAZUO, *Yamaguchi-gumi Third Generation*, Tokuma Shoten, Tokyo, 1973.

TERESA, VINCENT, *My Life in the Mafia*, Doubleday, New York, 1973.

TOLAND, JOHN, *The Rising Sun*, Random House, New York, 1970.

PERIODICALS AND NEWSPAPERS OF VARIOUS YEARS, including *Newsweek, Time, Tokyo Total, Asahi Shimbun, Daily Mainichi, Japan Times, Daily Yomiuri, Herald-Tribune, New York Times, London Times.*

POLICE FILES AND RESEARCH REPORT, NATIONAL POLICE AGENCY AND MUNICIPAL POLICE AGENCY, JAPAN.